AF622102

LULL AFTER THE STORM

(Poverty and Integrated Rural Development)

LULL AFTER THE STROM

(Poverty and Integrated Rural Development)

NADEEM MOHSIN

Commonwealth

Lull After The Strom

© NADEEM MOHSIN

ISBN : 81-7169-035-1

Edition : 2026

Published by :
COMMONWEALTH PUBLISHERS (P) LTD.
4831/24, Govind Lane,
Ansari Road, Darya Ganj,
New Delhi - 110002
Ph. : 23272541, 23242541
e-mail : commonwealthpublishers2016@gmail.com

Distributed by :
ARJUN PUBLISHING HOUSE
4831/24, Govind Lane,
Ansari Road, Darya Ganj,
New Delhi - 110002
Ph. : 23272541, 23242541
e-mail : arjunbooks2001@gmail.com

Laser Typesetting by :
Dimple Computers
Delhi

Printed at :
Divine Digital Press
Delhi

Dedicated to

My Parents
who have been divinely gifted
with a concern for all

Preface

In October 1985, a novel scheme of Concurrent Evaluation of Integrated Rural Development Programme was launched by the Ministry of Agriculture, Department of Rural Development, Government of India. An all India survey was conducted by reputed institutions from all over the country. The survey for Bihar was assigned to A. N. Sinha Institute of Social Studies, besides Xavier Institute of Social Service, Ranchi. The first phase of evaluation covered the period from October 1985 to September 1986. The second phase was started in January 1987 and continued till December. The third phase has just begun.

The present work embodies the result of an analysis of the main findings incorporated in the report of the second phase of evaluation. It includes data pertaining to the whole country and is expected to contribute to the formulation of subsequent evaluations and also aid policy decisions relating to poverty alleviation, an important component of the Eighth Five Year Plan objectives.

The author expresses his indebtedness to Raghunath Jha and Chandrapal Singh for collecting data for Bihar and to the Ministry for allowing, in principle, the institutions to use the data for research purposes. He is thankful to Prof. Pradhan H. Prasad for carefully going through the work and for writing a foreword, in spite of his extremely busy schedules. He also expresses thanks to Dr. M.P. Pandey for providing administrative assistance during data collection and to Prof. D.D. Guru, Dr. I.D. Sharma, Dr. A.N. Sharma, Dr. Jagdish Prasad, Dr. Shaibal Gupta, Dr. R. P. Sinha, Dr. M. B. Prasad, Dr. P.P. Ghosh and others in the Institute for their cooperation. He extends thanks to Dr. S.F. Rab, Mr. Nehal Ashraf and Yusuf for their assistance rendered in course of the library work. He is extremely thankful to Prof. Nurul Huda for having gone through the manuscript. He also owes a special debt of gratitude to his father, Prof. S.M. Mohsin.

The author is highly grateful for the cooperation extended by the bank officials, government functionaries and the beneficiaries in the conduct of the survey. They enriched the author by their valuable experiences and interesting anecdotes, some of which were of academic significance from the author's point of view.

The author acknowledges his wife's appreciation of the enduring pursuit entailed by this work. She often had to bear the brunt of his excessive involvement during the writing stage. He had also been cheered, time and again, by the exuberant presence of his daughter Alfia and son Sehran in course of writing this manuscript.

Lastly, the author expresses his thanks to Badri Prasad for typing the manuscript so meticulously.

A.N. Sinha Institute of
Social Studies, Patna-800001
August 1989.

Nadeem Mohsin

Foreword

Rural development in India has a fairly long history. The first few attempts to foster rural development were made at the non-governmental level in the early twentieth century. These were, however, fragmented efforts based on individual initiatives and were more on ideological rather than economic lines. It was the culmination of ideas set forth for the First Five Year Plan that really witnessed a breakthrough towards a concerted effort on rural development at the state level. The Community Development Programme was envisaged during the Plan as a major attempt to eradicate poverty and unemployment. Although a series of programmes followed thereafter in subsequent plans, it was the C.D. programme which had the rigour to continue on an everlasting basis, and within the broad contours of which the present poverty alleviation programmes have been formulated.

The Sixth and Seventh Plans launched special programmes for poverty alleviation, IRDP being the single largest amongst them. It is indeed perceived to be an attractive programme because of its subsidy component. Unfortunately, however, as the studies, by and large, reveal, such adhoc-based programmes have not been able to contribute much to the poor. Some findings suggest that they have, on the contrary, filled the coffers of a group of people who are much above the poverty level.

Although there is no dearth of literature on poverty alleviation through IRDP, cutting across extreme views, both in terms of its success and failures, this is perhaps the only detailed exercise in which an attempt has been made to examine the question of poverty at the all India level, incorporating the minutest components of the IRD programme. The study rightly concludes that IRDP in itself would not be able to solve the problem of poverty for years together, unless and until it is backed by fundamental institutional reforms and need-based strategies and becomes an integral part of the plan frame. The study also emphasises that the short-term objective of providing assets to the beneficiaries should go hand in hand with the long-term goal of transformation of economic and social structure in the rural areas.

The author has given a neat account of the rural development strategies followed in India from the pre-independence period. The analysis of the functioning of IRDP provides sufficient insight into the methodological issues involved in the programme. Furthermore, it highlights the administrative bottlenecks associated with it as well as its implementation loopholes. Some of the suggestions given by the author can be extremely useful from the standpoint of policy formulation.

Director,
A.N. Sinha Institute of
Social Studies, Patna.

Pradhan H. Prasad

Contents

List of Tables

1

A Profile of Poverty

The Initial Strategy

India on the eve of its independence, was carrying over the legacies of the British rule as a result of which a serious impasse took place in its endeavours for development.[1] Besides, it faced an economic environment in which mass poverty was almost in an endemic form.[2] The task before the planners, therefore, was enormously stupendous from the very beginning. The building up of an economy through democratic means and the establishment of a social order based upon justice and equality of opportunity was by no means an easy task.[3] In the words of the Government Resolution of March 1950, planning in fact was intended "to promote a rapid rise in the standard of living of the people by efficient exploitation of the natural resources of the country, increasing production, and offering opportunities to all for employment in the service of the country."[4]

With such an emphasis on a planned economic development and balanced growth, India from the very start adopted the policies fairly typical of so many developed countries of the world.[5] The initial phase of development was of an increasing food production and raw materials as a prerequisite for industrialisation. The second phase was a concentration on industrial development, and the third phase was a stress on the rapid increase of agricultural output, as a base for other sectors and for building self-reliance, all to the utter disregard of distributional aspects. The current phase is the rhetoric shift towards the transformation of the mass rural sector through the resources channelised for the benefit of the small farmers by means of labour-intensive rural projects, so as to generate extensive avenues of employment and rural infrastructure.[6]

The strategy adopted by India at the early stages of development did not bear fruit to the desired extent. Although the Gross National Product (GNP) increased over the years, the share of gains was not equitable. The three past phases of development referred to above, thus concentrated on the growth-centred strategy which was an imitation of the West. The successful planning models of the developed Western World were too readily adopted as ideal and appropriate to the developing countries.[7] The experiences of a few countries like Korea, Taiwan and Israel, which were cited repeatedly in the past as an evidence that high growth rates can be combined with equity are no longer tenable. A far greater equality of opportunity prevailed in these countries combined with a very high growth rate.[8] It is thus increasingly apparent that to rely on a rapid rate of growth in the GNP is not enough to hope that it would eventually filter down to the masses.[9] Hence the question of poverty cannot be solved if we simply stick to our old stereotyped "top-down, non-participative, harmony-based approach to rural development."[10]

Let us now pause and recollect the poverty scenario of the past four decades. It will surely help us rectify our errors without which we cannot possibly move ahead. Although there are evidences to show that the development strategies in the fifties and in the sixties concentrated on the growth-centred approach and overemphasized the role of the GNP as an indicator of growth, a mention of which has been made earlier, an ILO study expresses serious doubts about the success of such a strategy. It opines that rural development cannot be viewed as a narrow technical problem or as a means of increasing production through modern inputs.[11] Due importance was given to social progress and distributive justice even in the First Five Year Plan which viewed economic planning as an integral part of a wider process aiming not merely at the development of resources in a narrow technical sense, but also at the development of human facilities and at the building up of an institutional framework adequate to the needs and aspirations of the people.[12] The First Plan qualified its commitments to social justice and equality with its adherence to the dominant view prevailing at that time that rapid economic growth and income redistribution are irreconcilable and that the latter would occur in the later stages of development. On the contrary, it was feared that an overemphasis on equality could jeopardise development itself.[13] Stalwarts like Kenneth Boulding have supported the view that in a poor society, economic growth may require quite sharp inequalities and too great equality may condemn the society to stagnation.[14] Such fears are expressed in the First Plan itself: "It is important to ensure that the measures, fiscal and other, to be adopted for promoting economic equality do not dislocate production and jeopardise the prospects of ordered growth."[15]

Awareness of the Problem

The awareness of the problem of poverty in India dates back to 1870, when Dadabhai Naoroji first expressed his concern in an article on 'The Wants and Means of India.'[16] In 1876, Dadabhai wrote a book entitled: 'Poverty and Un-British Rule in India.'[17] In 1898, Lord Dufferin, Governor General, ordered an enquiry which was to determine whether or not the greater proportion of India suffered from a daily insufficiency of food.[18] Gandhi's campaigns in favour of the Harijans too was an exercise on the eradication of poverty. Soon after independence, the situation of landless labourers was carefully studied and their problems were incorporated in the First Plan as a part of the planning process. Thirty-one per cent of the total outlay was allocated for agriculture and irrigation.[19] During the Second Plan, the emphasis shifted to industrialisation for which the allocation was increased from 4 per cent during the First Plan to 20 per cent of the outlay, while the allocation for agriculture and irrigation was reduced from 31 per cent in the First Plan to 20 per cent of the outlay in the Second Plan,[20] thus giving equal weightage both to the agricultural as well as the industrial sector during this Plan.

Although the emphasis on the reduction of inequality was gaining ground with a thrust on the socialist ideology of an equitable distribution of economic gains, the 'growth first' policy advocated by Rostow[21] gained greater validity. This was further corroborated in Kuznet's legitimacy of widening gaps in the initial stages of development.[22] Although the industrialisation phase continued through the Third Plan, the debate between growth and social justice continued unabated. The Fourth Plan witnessed a major shift from industry to agriculture as a result of the effects of the HYV seed-fertiliser technology. Even though this technology achieved a major agricultural breakthrough in certain pocketed areas and led to an increase in the income of a selected few,[23] it also paved the way for an increased income inequality both inter-regional as well as intra-regional.[24] It was owing to the apprehension of a further increase in inequality which went against the basic dogma of growth with social justice, that the Fourth Plan reiterated its stand and stated: "to some extent income disparities can be reduced by fiscal measures aiming at reduction of income at the top levels, but for us it is important to lay far greater stress on positive steps for ameliorating the conditions of the poorer people through planned economic development."[25] The positive steps in the Plan referred to the infrastructural facilities, especially to the category of agricultural labourers, poor and middle farmers in rural areas, the lack of which created innumerable loopholes in the development endeavours of these groups. This lacuna in the Fourth Plan was nearly rectified in the Fifth Plan which declared removal of poverty and attainment of self-reliance as its main objectives. A new component of the Plan was a national programme for minimum needs such as elementary education, water supply and health care services. Both agriculture and industry were given emphasis from the growth and output point of view.[26] In the Draft Sixth Plan, a revised programme on minimum needs was formulated and a new section entitled: 'Distributive Justice' was added to it, which in itself is noteworthy even though supporting provisions in the Plan appear to be grossly inadequate.[27] The Sixth Plan clearly had a rural orientation. The outlay on agriculture and irrigation was to the extent of 26 per cent of the total outlay. The outlay on industry was a mere 15 per cent. The Plan accorded the highest priority to sectors "which generate the maximum employment and which have a significant impact on the standard of living of the poorest, like agriculture and allied activities, village and small industries."[28] The important growth rates were brought down from the usual targeted 5 to 7 per cent of the previous Plan to a more realistic 4.7 per cent. The two guiding considerations for these decisions are significant. First, the pattern of investment and therefore of income generation in the Plan should be such as to redistribute incomes in favour of the poor. Secondly, the physical targets should be projected with a greater degree of realism than in the past.[29] With a change in the Government, a revised Sixth Plan (1980-85) was formulated having a section on 'Social Justice'. The Plan concludes: "a greater degree of distribution bias has to be built into our development effort."[30] The approach to the Seventh Plan (1985-90) reiterates the goal of bringing down the percentage of population below the poverty line to less than ten by 1994 95.[31] It probably justifies this optimism through its massive allocation to the programmes of poverty alleviation. However, it fails to take count of the inherent deficiencies in the implemention of these programmes where all the 't's are not properly crossed and the 'i's properly dotted.[32] The impact of planning on rural poverty during the last three decades has been rather minimal. We cannot hope for better results in the near future considering the state of Indian polity and we cannot expect something miraculous from the Seventh Plan.

Magnitude of the Problem

There is no dearth of literature on poverty in India. The studies on poverty trends indicate two related phenomena: an intensification of inequality between the higher income group and poverty group as well as an increase in the overall incidence of poverty computed on the basis of income levels for basic calorie requirements. The highest 5 per cent income earners receive 22 per cent of national income, while the bottom 40 per cent receive less than 16 per cent of the income.[33] This trend was visible even in the seventies when the upper groups showed an increase in per capita consumption expenditure, the lower groups remained stagnant, while the bottom 5 per cent showed a decline.[34] During the past two decades, several studies have been made on the incidence of poverty in India. Among the studies that provide some time series data on the extent of poverty for the period upto 1967-68 or so, four are well known, viz., Dandekar and Rath (1971), Minhas (1970), Bardhan (1970-71) and Vaidyanathan (1971).[35] Two of them namely Dandekar-Rath and Bardhan have concluded that the proportion of rural population below the poverty line increased between 1960-61 and 1967-68, while Minhas and Vaidyanathan have come to the conclusion that the proportion of people below the poverty line has declined during this period. Based on the original estimates of the NSS data on consumer expenditure for the year 1967-68 as compared with those for 1960-61, Dandekar and Rath could not find that poverty had relatively increased; so they made adjustments in the NSS estimate of per capita consumption for only the year 1967-68 on the ground that the expenditure estimate was more than 10 per cent below the official estimate based on national income aggregates, and they attributed this to the possible tendency that the upper middle and richer households have become increasingly inaccessible to the NSS investigators.[36] There are also studies on poverty by Panikar,[37] Sukhamte,[38] and Scott[39] which hold diverging views about the incidence of poverty in India. However there appears, by and large, a consensus on two aspects: first that the percentage of population below the poverty line has not decreased despite three decades of planning on the ideals of a just and equitable distribution of income; and second that the absolute number of persons below the poverty line has certainly increased by large numbers during the period.[40] This has been summarized by the Planning Commission in the Draft Sixth Plan:[41]

> "Attempts have been made to measure the extent of poverty in India and depending on the norms used, 40-60 per cent of the population fall below the minimum acceptable standard. According to a recent estimate using norms of calorie consumption, the percentage of population below the poverty line in 1977-78 may be projected at 48 per cent in rural areas and 41 per cent in urban areas. The total number of poor so defined would be about 290 million. Though these estimates are debatable, it cannot be doubted that we have a long way to go to ensure a tolerable standard of living for a large number of the poor and the destitute. The prevalence of poverty and inequality has remained virtually unchanged over the years. Trends in the distribution of income and wealth are difficult to discern, but the evidence of persistence of gross inequalities is clear. The distribution of assets for rural household shows that 20 per cent of the households each having less than Rs. 1000 worth of assets, account for less than one per cent of all rural assets, while 4 per cent with asset values of Rs. 50,000 or more own over 30 per cent of the assets."

Talking of the magnitude of poverty in India, however, stems down to mere mind-boggling. No matter how many poor there are in countries like India, the problem is so grave that for a long time to come no efforts made to solve it can be superfluous.[42] Poverty need not always be measured; it needs to be prevented and abolished.[43]

Notes and References

1. Prasad, Pradhan H., "Poverty and agricultural development", Economic and Political Weekly, Dec. 14, 1985. Also see Prasad's "Agrarian Violence in Bihar", Economic and Political Weekly,

May 30, 1987 and "Institutional reforms and agricultural growth", Social Scientist, June, 1986.

2. Bagchi, Amiya K., The Political Economy of Underdevelopment, Cambridge University Press, 1982, p. 91.
3. Third Five Year Plan, Planning Commission, Government of India, New Delhi, p. 4.
4. Fourth Five Year Plan, Planning Commission, Government of India, New Delhi, p. 2.
5. Brara, J.S., The Political Economy of Rural Development, Allied Publishers Private Limited, New Delhi, 1983, p. 16.
6. Ibid., p. 16.
   See also Lipton, Michael, Why People Stay Poor, Temple Smith, London, 1976.
7. Mohsin, Nadeem, Rural Development Through Government Programmes, Mittal Publishing Company, New Delhi, 1985, p. 1.
8. Haq, Mahbub Ul, The Poverty Curtain, Oxford University Press, 1979, p. 61.
9. Ibid., p. 55.
10. Sethi, Harsh, "Rural development : alternative strategies", in Arvind N. Das and V. Nilakant ed., Agrarian Relations in India, Manohar Publications, New Delhi, 1979, p. 95.
11. See the ILO study conducted by Dharam Ghai, Azizur Rahman Khan, Ed. Lee and Samir Radwan, entitled, Agrarian Systems and Rural Development, London, 1979, p. 1.
12. First Five Year Plan, Planning Commission, Government of India, 1952, p. 7.
13. Op. cit. (5), p. 16.
14. Boulding, Kenneth, Economic Analysis, Harper and Bros., New York, 1941, p. 724.
15. See the summary report on the First Five Year Plan, Planning Commission, Government of India, 1952.
16. Etienne, Gilbert, India's Changing Rural Scene, Oxford University Press, Delhi, 1982, p. 195.
17. The description of this is given in Dantwala's Poverty in India : Then and Now, New Delhi, 1973.
18. Bhatia, B.M., Famines in India, 1860-1945, London, 1963, p. 145.
19. See the Draft Five Year Plan, 1978-83, Planning Commission, Government of India, p. 17.
20. Ibid.
21. Rostow has nicely defended his 'growth first' theory in his book : The Stages of Economic Growth, Cambridge University Press, 1962.

22. Kuznets, Simon, "Economic growth and income inequality", American Economic Review, March 1955, See note 10.

23. See Hopper, David, "Allocation efficiency in traditional Indian agriculture", Journal of Farm Economics, 47(3), 1965, pp. 611-624. Also see Chenna Reddy, V., "Production efficiency in South Indian agriculture", Journal of Farm Economics, 49(4), 1967, pp. 816-821; Mellor, J.W., Economics of Agriculturul Production, Cornell University Press, Ithaca, 1966, pp. 133-135; Ghosh, R.N., Agriculture in Economic Development with Special Reference to Punjab, Vikas Publishing House, Private Ltd., New Delhi, 1979, p. 49; Bhalla, G.S., Changing Agrarian Structure in India, Meenakshi Publications, Meerut, 1974, p. 2; Sen, Sudhir, Reaping the Green Revolution: Food and Jobs for All, Tata McGraw Hill Co., New Delhi, 1975; Sarkar, P.C., The Planning of Indian Agriculture, Rotterdam University Press, 1966; Christensen, R.P., "Agricultural progress in less developed countries," in Economic Development of Agriculture, Iowa State University Press, USA., 1965, p. 25: Frankel, F.R., India's Green Revolution: Economic Gains and Political Costs, Princeton University Press, New Jersey, 1971; Prasad, Pradhan H., Economic benefits in the Kosi Command Area," A.N. Sinha Institute of Social Studies, Mimeograph, Patna, 1979.

24. See Dantwala, M.L., "Agricultural policy in India since independence," Indian Journal of Agricultural Economics, No. 4, Oct. Dec. 1976, p. 41. Also see Ashok Mitra, "Bumper harvest has created some dangerous illusions," The Statesman, Oct. 14-15, 1988; Mishra, G.P., "The green revolution—changes and challenges," Eastern Economist, September 1973; Rao, C.H.H., "Farm size and credit policy," Economic and Political Weekly, Dec. 26, 1970; Chowdhry, B.K., Disparity in income in the context of H.Y.V.," Economic and Political Weekly, Sept. 26, 1970; Rudhra, A., "Big Farmers in Punjab," Economic and Political Weekly, Dec. 27, 1969; Mellor, J.W., Report on "Technological advance in Indian agriculture, as it relates to the distribution of income," Dec. 12, 1969; Bal, H.S. and Gurbachan Singh, "Pattern of income distribution in rural areas," Indian Journal of Agricultural Economics, Vol. XXV, No. 3, July-Sept. 1970.

25. Fourth Five Year Plan, Planning Commission, Government of India, New Delhi, 1970, p. 14.

26. For details, consult Draft Outline of the Fifth Five Year Plan, Planning Commission, Government of India, New Delhi, 1974.

27. Raj Krishna, the main author of the major policy chapters of the Sixth Plan including the one on 'Distributive Justice', said in an interview that the measures for distributive justice were diluted and watered down by the previous Janata Government and

the majority in the Planning Commission. For the average low level of growth, the Government has become irrelevant and for distributive justice, the Government is indifferent. Sunday, Sept. 9, 1979, pp. 34-38.

28. Draft outline of the Sixth Five Year Plan, Planning Commission, Government of India, 1978-83, p. 17.
29. Ibid., p. 6.
30. Sixth Five Year Plan, 1980-85, Planning Commission, Government of India, New Delhi, 1980, p. 7.
31. Seventh Five Year Plan, 1985-90, Planning Commission, Government of India, New Delhi, 1985, p. 50.
32. Mohsin, Nadeem, "Integrated rural development programme and poverty alleviation", in Sharma and Gupta ed. **Bihar : Stagnation or Growth**, Spectrum Publishers, New Delhi, 1987, p. 100.
33. Op. cit. (5), p. 20.
34. Dandekar, V.M. and N. Rath, "Poverty in India—dimensions and trends", Economic and Political Weekly, Jan. 2 and 9, 1971.
35. Shetty, S.L., "Structural retrogression in the Indian Economy since the mid sixties", Economic and Political Weekly, Vol. XIII, Nos. 6-7, Feb. 1978, p. 211.
36. Dandekar, V.M. and N. Rath, Poverty in India, The Ford Foundation, New Delhi, Dec. 1970, p. 37.
37. Panikar, P.G., "Economics of nutrition", Economic and Political Weekly, Annual Number, Feb. 1972.
38. Sukhamte, P.V., "Incidence of Undernutrition", Indian Journal of Agricultural Economics, No. 3, 1977. Also see his article, "Assessment of adequacy of diets at different income levels", Economic and Political Weekly, Vol. XIII, Nos. 31, 32 and 35, Aug. 1978, p. 1373. Sukhamte's arguments have been corroborated in N. Krishnaji's article of May 30, 1981, Economic and Political Weekly,p. 989, and Sept. 12, 1981, Economic and Political Weekly, p. 1509; D. Banerji's article of Sept. 26, 1981, Economic and Political Weekly, p. 1579.
39. Scott, W., Concepts and Measurement of Poverty, Geneva, 1981.
40. Op. cit. (5), p. 22.
41. Draft Five Year Plan, 1978-83, Planning Commission, Government of India, p. 3.
42. Op. cit. (16); Also see Jain, L.C. et.al., Grass Without Roots, Sage Publications, New Delhi, 1985.
43. Op. cit. (4), p. 7.

2

Rural Development in Retrospect

Rural development in India has had a fairly long history going back to several decades before independence. Over the years, it has emerged as a strategy designed to improve the economic and social life of a specific group of people, the rural poor.[1] It involves extending the benefits of development to the poorest among those who seek a livelihood in the rural areas.[2] It aims at the optimum utilization of the natural and human resources of a given rural area for the enrichment of the quality of life of its population.[3] The main objective of rural development thus has been the elimination of poverty which has continued unabated for years on end.

Pre-independence Efforts

Some of the early experiments on rural development date back to the early twenties and thirties of the century. The Sriniketan and Santiniketan experiments of Rabindranath Tagore, the Martandam project of Spencer Hatch of the YMCA and Brayne's Gurgaon experiment were initiated as early as 1921. Krishnamachari's Baroda rural reconstruction movement was started in the early thirties. Mahatma Gandhi also initiated various experiments, especially in Champaran in 1917 and at Sevagram in 1936.

Data on early experiments unfortunately are scanty. Very few systematic, objective appraisals of these experiments were conducted during the early implementation stages.[4] There were articles and books written by social workers associated with these experiments. However, the tendency among them was to emphasize the philosophy and ideals of these experiments and the approach and processes involved in them, and give some illustrations of certain startling or unusual events. Little or no information was provided on the financial aspects of these experiments: sources of funds, investments, breakup of costs, financial returns, increase in net income of farmers and others, direct and invisible costs of social welfare activities; extent to which economic activities were self-generating, etc. As such, we really know very little about the actual nature of these experiments.[5]

Some studies, however, give an insight into the type of social activities undertaken, the persons involved in these activities, their perception of rural problems and needs, their approach to these problems, etc. The major emphasis underlying these activities was on the philosophical aspects of the experiments so much so that the economic and social objectives behind these activities were set aside. These experiments were conducted under the colonial rule. Indian thinking during that period lacked both depth and vision devoid of any scientific and technological perspective. Economic and commercial orientations were least visible. Social reformers and educationists like Tagore and Gandhi were conspicuous by their presence but economic giants and scientists were not there. Scientific temper and technological advancement did not seem to stir the minds of social thinkers. Besides this, British rule did not encourage or tolerate ideas or experiments that came in the way of its basic interest in subjugating the mass of the rural populace and exploiting the national and human resources of the colony for its own benefit. The early experiments on rural development, which were more humanistic and philosophical did not carry any germs of technological revolution from the developed Western world to the Indian countryside. They were tolerated by the British and often at times encouraged by them. It was for this reason that these experiments were not managed by Indians alone. A number of well-meaning, socially-oriented Westerners initiated and contributed substantially to the management of these experiments.[6] For example, C.F. Andrews was involved in Tagore's Sarul experiments.[7] Leonard Elmhirst played a pivotal role in the Sriniketan experiment;[8] Dr. Spencer Hatch managed the Martandam project of the YMCA for 18 years;[9] the Gurgaon scheme was initiated by F.L. Brayne;[10] the Etawah Pilot Project was initiated and managed by Albert Mayor.[11] Seeing the involvement of the foreigners in the early experiments, it can be said without an iota of doubt that the influence of foreigners on the design of rural development has been substantial during the pre-independence period.[12] Let us discuss the salient features of these experiments.

From the earlier writings of Tagore we get the glimpses of how his sensitive philosophical mind perceived the rural scene not in isolation but in a variety of perspectives.[13] Tagore's concern was confined not merely to the immediate sufferings of the masses. Like many sages in the past, he thought of much larger issues faced by human society towards the perception of ultimate realities similar to the teachings of the Upanishads.[14] Mukerji observed that both Tagore and Gandhi knew that India lived in villages, both wanted villages to be the growth-cones of India, both believed in decentralised economy, and both wanted Swaraj (self-rule).[15] However, both failed to point out the way of absorbing the technological evolution that took place in the West and that could come as a boon to India. This opposition to science, technology, and industrialisation and emphasis on the spiritual aspects of life found predominance in Tagore's experiments in education as well as in many other earlier experiments. Tagore's efforts, however, failed[16] since his approach was one of an educationist and a philosopher. The Santiniketan experiment of Tagore had little to do with rural development per se for the first twenty years. His basic idea behind this experiment was to spread education in a rural setting, for which he recruited the services of an Englishman Leonard Elmhirst. Over the years,

Sriniketan became a centre of many institutions for research, extension and education. It maintained a demonstration farm, a dairy and poultry unit, an outdoor clinic, a department of cottage industries, and a village school. These agencies were to treat the villages as their laboratory to identify problems and test their ideas. The villagers were expected to approach these agencies through the village workers to obtain solution of their more pressing problems. The social worker lived in the village in isolation, working with the people and neither 'for them' nor 'on behalf of them'.[17]

Although the Santiniketan experiment paved the way for a brighter future among the villagers, it met only with partial success. The experiment in practice was reduced to keeping a section of people permanently rural, completely bound to agriculture. In the entire scheme there were no efforts to develop those enterprises which could work as a driving force to economic progress. This was because of the value system as well as the background of the social workers involved in the experiment. They could not think of any new enterprises which would provide such a driving force; they could also not think in terms of exploiting the natural resources which remain unutilised, generating employment opportunities, creating demand and developing new skills, etc. These social workers could, at best, contribute only a little bit to literacy and health facilities. Very little effort was made to use the technologies already in operation in Western countries which could change the form of Indian agriculture, making it more modern, and thereby reducing the drudgery of all those people physically involved in it. In short, the experiment was weak on many fronts: its purpose, the value system it was trying to inculcate, the approach, the personnel, the programmes, the activities, planning, implementation, etc. It could not, thus, be a model for rural reconstruction.

Just when the Sriniketan experiment was being initiated in eastern India by Elmhirst, another project on rural development was taking shape at Martandam, near Trivandrum in South India under the leadership of Dr. Spencer Hatch, an

American.[18] Dr. Hatch, together with the then Indian General Secretary of the National Council of the YMCAs, Mr. K Paul, opened up a rural reconstruction centre at Mart The main programmes taken up at the Centre revolved people's welfare through their own efforts, the concept h resemblance to the later developed idea of Community lopment. Like the Sriniketan experiment, however, this project also dealt in easily identifiable, stereotype activities like bee-keeping, improved poultry and cows, handicrafts and literacy. These could, at best, provide marginal gains to some families. The programme and activities were, nevertheless, better organised than Sriniketan, due to the organisational strength of the YMCA.

The Gurgaon scheme in northern India was a contemporary of Sriniketan and Martandam.[19] Towards the end of 1920, Mr. F.L. Brayne, an Englishman, was posted as Deputy Commissioner of Gurgaon district. Brayne took unusual interest in the welfare of the rural people and made extensive tours in the villages to study the conditions of the people. After about seven years of study and experiment, Brayne evolved a scheme called 'The Gurgaon Scheme'. In 1925, a school of rural economy was set up for training of village guides. The village guides were trained with the purpose of developing cooperatives, taking up public health work, cleaning of villages by digging of manure pits, putting in windows, ventilators in the houses, and demonstrating and selling improved ploughs and other implements, improved seeds, etc. In 1926, a Domestic School of Economy was set up. This was managed by Miss E.M. Wilson, an English woman. The idea was to train a group of women in Women and Child Welfare work. The school had a provision of primary teaching, apart from lessons on sewing, knitting, cutting, embroidery, toymaking, cooking, hygiene, sanitation, first aid and child welfare, etc. A health association was also formed which ran five health centres in the district. The nurses at these centres also acted as health guides. Local women received training in midwifery. A Women's Institute was also set up at Gurgaon to manage the ladies' garden in Gurgaon and to organise ...s, lectures, first aid classes, etc.

...s regards the results of the Gurgaon Scheme, Verma ...s, "It marked a definite departure in the technique of ... improvement and attracted India-wide attention. It ...d grand, but alas, it was not to last long or take roots."[20] Elmhirst, Hatch and Brayne were contemporaries. Brayne's approach and activities were similar to those of the other two. All were concerned about those things in rural India which offended the eye and nose of the urbanites, especially the foreigners. None of them were concerned about the more serious problems of abject poverty engulfing their areas of operation. In Brayne's project, there was no coordination between agriculture production-oriented activities with output marketing which ultimately was the primary concern of farmers and village craftsmen, as his entire economy depended on the marketing of his produce.

The Baroda experiment was started in the early thirties. Baroda was a princely state in Western India. Under the enlightened rule of Maharaja Sir Sivajirao Gaekwar, this state made considerable progress starting from the late 19th century in the field of education, agriculture and welfare as compared to many other princely states in British India.[21] Kavoori observes that the Raja believed in the leadership of the educated. During his rule he restored political and social stability. A number of basic amenities and other development services were provided by him. Public works of various kinds, provision of medical services, irrigation, roads and transport provided basic amenities to rural people.[22] All these were the essential conditions for further development.[23] In these efforts, V.T. Krishnamachari played an important role. Under him, agriculture became the heart of rural development. Notable work was done in this area, especially the introduction of rural reconstruction centres with the help of Dr. Spencer Hatch of the YMCA.

The Baroda experiment was not an experiment in the sense that Sriniketan and Martandam were. It was not limited to a few villages and to a few activities. Its social programme covered the entire State, and the economic development programmes intensively covered hundreds of villages spread over all the districts of the State. It covered human development, organisational infrastructure and legislative support. The major contribution of the Baroda State's efforts was in the field of mass education. The emphasis on agricultural production through demonstration, extension and training did help in creating a general awareness among farmers about new varieties and practices. However, there is little evidence that fifty years of efforts in strengthening the cooperative movement and agricultural development made the economy of the villages of Baroda State substantially better than that of other provinces.[24] The approach to the Baroda experiment itself carried the germs of failure. Considering rural reconstruction mainly in terms of literacy, welfare, civic amenities, cottage industries, agriculture, and credit cooperatives has not been very effective in transforming the society. There was no force in these activities, individually or collectively which could move the society on the path of economic progress.

Gandhi's experiments outclassed others if one were to take into consideration the motivation, objectives, scope and activities of his experiments. To have a clear understanding of his programmes one has to bear in mind two things : First, he was primarily a political strategist whose main objective was to take India out of the fetters of British rule. As such, all his actions have to be viewed in terms of a particular socio-economic perspective. Secondly, each of his actions was a singular blend of two components : a simple looking outward act with tremendous mass appeal, and the sanctity of an inward principle which governed his spirits. In 1917, he started his experiment in Champaran. The emphasis was on child and adult education. Adults were taught hygiene, road construction work, digging of wells, etc. by his team workers. At Champaran, for the first time, he actually offered passive resistance in order to remedy the evils connected with indigo plantations. He also launched the programmes of Village Swaraj (self-rule) and Swadeshi (indigenous) movement.

Under these programmes, he introduced extremely simple activities such as Charkha (spinning wheel) and Khadi (hand-made cloth), village sanitation and hygiene. In 1936, he settled at Sevagram, a village near Wardha. He served the villages by undertaking various activities like road sweeping, revival of handicrafts, introducing improved agricultural practices and new varieties of crops. Since Gandhi mixed with the untouchables and used excreta as manure, people in surrounding villages did not cooperate with him.[25] Gandhi advocated for a 'self-sufficient village economy' and 'self-reliant village community', and emphasized utilisation of local resources for development.[26] Compared to Gandhi's programme, other experiments were mere pygmies, and their failures made them still more insignificant.[27]

Post-independent Rural Development Strategies

The first and foremost programme of rural development after independence was launched by Albert Mayor, an American architect and a soldier in India at the time of the Second World War. Mayor made extensive tours of the villages of Uttar Pradesh and came up with the idea of a model village. During 1947-48, he found a team of four specialists—a town and village planner, an agricultural extension specialist, an agricultural engineer and a specialist in rural industries. On September 15, 1948, Mayor and his team submitted their Pilot Intensive Project for Etawah district in Uttar Pradesh. The project was started in October 1948 in Maheva village. The objectives of the project were :[28]

1. To know the extent of economic and social improvement, as well as of the initiative, self-confidence and cooperation that could be achieved in the villages of the district;
2. To find out how quickly these results could be attained;
3. To know whether the results remained a part of people's mental, spiritual and technical equipment and outlook; and

4. To assess how far the results were reproducible in other places.

The programme of work under the project was, by and large, similar to earlier projects : "introduction of improved variety of seeds, chemical fertilisers, green-manuring, compost-making, improved implements, irrigation, plant protection measures, horticultural development, soil conservation, improved cultural practices; animal husbandry through upgrading of cattle, disease control; provision of cooperative societies for credit, production, marketing and supply; better sanitation and health services, maternity and child welfare services; improvement of roads, water supply, drainage and other public utility works; improvement of housing, broad-based social education programmes by means of adult literacy classes, study tours, farmers' fairs, village leaders' training camps, mass contact programmes etc."[28] The Etawah Project design and results indicate that Mayor did not pay much attention to the results of earlier experiments, and repeated, more or less, the same approach, identical programmes and similar activities. There was no linkage between agriculture and industry. After the initial results which appeared spectacular the project failed to achieve its objectives.

Community Development Programme

The greatest achievement of the experiments conducted in different areas and at different points of time was that these experiments paved the way for a massive movement on the rural front on the eve of the First Five Year Plan. The major impetus for framing a programme of Community Development by Chester Bowles, an U.S. ambassador to India was provided by a multitude of forces—both domestic and foreign. The experience of the striking achievements of the extension experiments in the U.S. and the sporadic non-official experiments in rural reconstruction going on in India inspired our planners to accept the idea of the Community Development Projects and National Extension Service. Incidentally, at this very time, India was facing an annual food deficit of around three million tonnes which further accentuated the need for rural transformation. Since majority of the activities in the rural areas revolved around agriculture, rural reconstruction needed to be given top priority. The food deficit accruing in the country made the planners set up a 'Grow More Food' Enquiry Committee, which submitted its report in 1952. It elaborated the concept of Extension Service and observed :

> "It is that all aspects of rural life are interrelated and that no lasting results can be achieved if individual aspects of it are dealt with in isolation—the plans for them should form parts of and be integrated with those for achieving the wider aims. It is only by placing this idea of bringing about an appreciable improvement in the standards of rural life and making it fuller and richer before the country and ensuring that the energies of the entire administrative machinery of the states and the best unofficial leadership are directed to the plans for its realisation, that we can awaken mass enthusiasm and enlist the active interest and support of millions of families living in the country-side in the immense task of bettering their own conditions. What we have said points inevitably to the need of an organisation for intensive rural work which would reach every farmer and assist in the coordinated development of rural life as a whole. At the village level, there will be one worker for five to ten villages who will be the major agent for all development activities and who will convey to the farmer the lessons of research and to the experts the difficulties of the farmer and arrange the supplies and services needed by the farmer. The role of village worker will be vital in rural development."[30]

The Committee made the following basic recommendations :

(*i*) National Extension Service should be enforced throughout the country within the period of seven or eight years.

(ii) The 'Service' should be carried out with the help of both official and non-official agencies at different levels from State to village.

(iii) The central aid should be extended for establishment and running of the scheme.

This Committee proved to be the most effective body and its recommendations were examined for their feasibility in consultation with the State Governments. The Planning Commission after the signing of the Indo-American Technical Cooperation Agreement of 1952,[31] adopted an extensive programme of Community Development projects and 55 such projects all over India were inaugurated in October, 1952. These projects which were of the nature of pilot experiments, sought to undertake intensive operations spread over a period of three years. But as the improvement in rural areas is a permanent process,[32] the projects were supplemented by a less intensive scheme of development known as National Extension Service which was started all over India on October 2, 1953, and 259 Blocks were selected for the year 1953-54. The term Community Development relates to methods by which the people who live in local communities become involved in helping improve their economic and social conditions.[33] According to the United Nations Organisation, Community Development is the process by which the efforts of the people themselves are united with those of governmental authorities to improve the economic, social and cultural conditions so as to integrate these communities into the life of the nation and to enable them to contribute fully to natural progress.[34]

There is a popular confusion between Community Development and Extension Service in India. Community Development is designed to promote better living for the whole community with an active participation of, and if possible on the initiative of the community but if this initiative is not forthcoming from them the use of techniques for arousing and stimulating it in order to secure its active and enthusiastic response is to be made.[35] More specifically for India "Community Development is the method and Rural Extension the agency through which the Five Year Plan seeks to initiate the process of transformation of social and economic life of villagers."[36]

The Indian Community Development Programme as a whole represents an approach having four essential steps, in the following order :

(i) assessment of the nature of local problems and realization of people's needs,

(ii) finalisation of objectives—direction of development,

(iii) setting up of specific agencies to execute them, and

(iv) appointment of bodies to evaluate the results of the operations. This approach is inevitable so far as our basic principles of development are concerned. "Community development is the only route by which the people of India may eventually gain the knowledge, the feeling, the practice, and experience of making freedom a living reality while at the same time build an economy in which they may share the benefits of the twentieth century."[37]

Upto April, 1977, the programme had covered more than five thousand blocks all over the country and is continuing in its own way, with the major emphasis now being laid on block level planning.[38] According to V.T. Krishnamachari, the programme can be successful if the following conditions are determined :

(i) a careful organisation of programmes for improving all aspects of rural life;

(ii) increased agricultural prosperity:

(iii) the block team should exhibit unity, coordinate its activities and secure help from non-official leadership; and

(iv) provide enhanced role to the panchayat and co-operatives.[39]

Since these preconditions were absent, the Community Development Programme failed either to accelerate growth or to confer benefits on the poor to the extent desired. The failure is due to the difference of opinions about objectives, the absence of conditions that the programme has taken for granted and some defects in administrative arrangements.[40]

The reasons for failure or limited success of Community Development Programme have been further summarised as :

(i) absence of a rational criteria in grouping 100 villages into a block, or locating the block head-quarters;

(ii) the services provided at the block level were inadequate in quantity as well as quality to meet the needs of important villages;

(iii) the social structure of village society did not undergo much change and the institutional reforms were inadequate and poorly implemented;

(iv) the village and the cooperatives in the new faction-torn and caste-ridden institutions, did not show any interest in the programme; and

(v) the programme was, as a whole, largely oriented towards welfare rather than development.[41]

For such a gigantic programme there was no arrangement of priorities. The study of certain blocks spread all over India revealed that the programme is still seen as an official venture and the people depend on the Government to do things for them. Most respondents consider the Block Development Officer rather than their elected representative as the key man in the programme. This indicates that the programme remains external to the village.[42] In Nov. 1957, a Committee on Plan Projects observed that unless the people and their democratic institutions took full responsibility in the planning and supervision of the programmes the movement of Community Development would never reach the desired goal.[43] On the basis of this information in 1959, Panchayati Raj, a 3-tier system of decentralisation of power was introduced. Through Community Development Programmes and introduction of Panchayati Raj system, a 3-pronged attack was designed against stagnation and the perpetuation mechanism of the Indian Society. For a quick but steady economic recovery, agricultural and industrial programmes were initiated. Housing, transportation and communication, health and sanitation programmes were designed to promote a better way of life, and education and social welfare programmes were intended to tone up the society. In other words, Community Development Schemes in conjunction with the Panchayati Raj, were designed to make frontal attacks against the stagnation of society by planning economic take-off and elimination of socio-economic disparities. The Panchayati Raj System, in particular, was made responsible for bringing about a change in the locus of power in rural India, and of thus affecting redistribution of control over rescurces and for stabilising such changes.[44]

Intensive Agricultural District Programme

While democratic decentralisation was being introduced at one level, there were parallel moves within the Government initiating a shift away from the community, or towards an area development concept in favour of a sectoral, professional (no involvement with community) approach. In 1959, the Government appointed a Ford Foundation sponsored team of experts on 'India's Food Crisis,' following disappointment with the Community Development Programme's performance in raising agricultural production.[45]

The team of experts was optimistic about the capacity and ability of Indian farmers and soil to raise agricultural production. It, however, recommended the selection of certain crops and certain areas for more intensive efforts. In other words, the team suggested that certain areas with assured water supply and with high potential for rapid increase in food production should be taken up for intensive cultivation, and in order to maximise food production the farmers of such areas were to be provided with adequate materials and services at the right time. The points suggested by the team were :[46]

1. Adequate farm credit based on production potential, made readily accessible through strengthened cooperatives.
2. Adequate supplies of fertilisers, pestieides, improved seeds, improved farm implements and other essential production needs made readily accessible through strengthened cooperatives.
3. Price incentives to participating cultivators through assured price agreements for rice, wheat, and millets announced two years in advance.
4. Marketing arrangements and services which enable the cultivator to obtain the full market prices for his marketed surplus.
5. Intensive educational, technical, and farm management assistance made available to every village in every development block in the district.
6. Participation of all interested cultivators, both large and small, in direct individual farm planning for increased food production.
7. Village planning for increased production, and village programmes, strengthening of village organisations and village leadership.
8. A public works programme, using local labour to undertake drainage, bunding, soil conservation, minor irrigation, building of approach roads and other development works contributing directly to increased production.
9. Analysis and evaluation of the programme from its inception.
10. Coordination on a priority basis by village, block, district, State and Centre, of all resources essential for carrying out the programme with maximum speed and effectiveness.

Subsequently, the suggestions except the one regarding incentives were approved by the Government of India and the Intensive Agricultural District Programme (IADP) moved from mere idea to implementation and action stage, in 1960. The suggestion regarding public works programme although accepted was not implemented in direct connection with IADP.

The IADP was included in the Third Plan, which states :

> "In pursuance of this proposal, the intensive agricultural district programme has been taken up, to begin with, in one district in each State. The programme is intended to contribute both to rapid increase in agricultural production in selected areas and to suggest new innovations and combination of practices which may be of value elsewhere."[47]

To make the IADP effective, the Third Plan went on to say :

> "An attempt will be made to provide all the essential elements for increasing production to the extent needed; an effort will be made to provide credit on a scale sufficient to reach all farmers, including those previously considered uncredit-worthy, and credit and marketing will be linked."[48]

Thus, IADP was set up to develop the whole farm community. It was intended that the IADP would work out a programme that both speeded up agricultural production and at the same time carried the programme to all farmers small as well as large, tenants as well as owners of agricultural lands. It would combine all efforts into one programme for general economic development of the area in which it operated.

In 1959, seven States were asked to select one district each for the launching of the programme. These were Andhra Pradesh, Bihar, Madhya Pradesh, Madras (now Tamil Nadu), Punjab, Uttar Pradesh and Rajasthan. The districts selected for the implementation of the IADP were expected to fulfil the following conditions :

(a) The district should, as far as possible, have assured water supply;

(b) It should have minimum of natural hazards, i.e., there should not be problems requiring long-term attention, such as susceptibility to floods, drainage problems, acute soil conservation problems, etc;

(c) It should, as far as possible, have well developed village institutions like cooperatives and panchayats;

(d) It should have maximum potentialities for increasing agricultural production within a comparatively short time.

It was presumed that adequate research results were available to bring about appreciable increase in agricultural production in the selected districts.

The State Governments selected the following districts for the implementation of the programme :

Thanjavur in Tamil Nadu	(Kharif 1960-61)
West Godavari in Andhra Pradesh	(Rabi 1960-61)
Shahabad (now Bhojpur and Rohtas) in Bihar	(Rabi 1960-61)
Raipur in Madhya Pradesh	(Kharif 1961-62)
Ludhiana in Punjab	(Kharif 1961-62)
Pali in Rajasthan	(Kharif 1961-62)

The programme was subsequently extended to other remaining States also so as to cover one district in each State and also to the Union Territory of Delhi (1964-65). After the formation of the new State of Haryana, IADP was started in Karnal district of the State (1967-69). The Governments of Rajasthan and Maharashtra, however, scaled down the IADP in Pali and Bhandara districts to the level of other intensive programmes in the States such as the Intensive Agricultural Area Programme (IAAP).

The original basis for the selection of IADP districts was the potential for increasing the production of the principal crop of the district. However, later on the programme was enlarged to include all crops in addition to the one for which the district was originally selected. But by the time this modified approach could be adopted, the districts had already been selected. Furthermore, in order to implement the programme without delay, the launching of the programme was done without adequate preparation so that even bench-mark surveys could not start prior to the launching of the programme.

The basic conditions laid down by the IADP for the selection of districts could not be completely satisfied by any of the districts, and in fact the condition of assured water supply could not be fully met by even a single district. The area classified as irrigated in all cases included a wide range of conditions from year round irrigation capable of supporting multiple cropping to just one or two supplemental irrigations in the rainy season itself. In a district like Raipur, the irrigated area though about 1.2 lakh hectares depends on the adequacy of the first monsoon rains and the irrigation is designed to supplement the rainfall, particularly in August-September. After September, the canals go dry. Similar is the case, more or less, of Shahabad district in Bihar. In Aligarh, the canal irrigation system could not meet the requirements of the high-yielding variety crops, as the available water had already been diverted to thousands of farms relatively thinly for meeting the requirements of traditional varieties. Moreover, most of the irrigation except from private wells and tubewells, is not controlled or regulated at the field level. Even in a district like Thanjavur, which has the largest area under irrigation, the irrigation is not controlled at this level and is not capable of being put fully to productive use. In West Godavari and in several other districts, the irrigation water is unregulated at the farm level. Even in a district which has comparatively better irrigation facilities these are confined only to a part of the district, and the rest of it depends on the vagaries of monsoon. For example, in West Godavari, only the delta area is favoured by irrigation from the Godavari canal network. The upland area is mostly rainfed.

The second condition for the selection of the district was that it should have a minimum of natural hazards, But even good districts like Thanjavur, West Godavari and Ludhiana have major drainage problems requiring long-term attention. Raipur and Pali, as experience shows, are subject to frequent droughts. Considerable parts of Aligarh, West Godavari and Thanjavur are subject to floods.

The third condition was that the selected district should have well developed village institutions like Cooperatives and Panchayats. Experience has shown that the Cooperatives in the districts did not have sufficient capabilities to give the needed support to intensive agricultural programmes. The Panchayati Raj institutions, too, were not developed enough to undertake a programme of this nature.

It is thus clear that although the IADP was launched in some of the best districts in the country, the conditions set for the programme could be only partially satisfied. In retrospect, it appears that this may not have been altogether unfortunate. The programme operated under some realistic and representative conditions of the farming areas of the country and thus encountered various problems usually faced by the farmers. This proved useful in its 'path-finder' or experimental role, although it often inhibited its 'pace-setting' or demonstrational role.[40] It was able to gather experience of working under diverse conditions from which valuable lessons were learnt.

Not only the criteria set for the selection of IADP districts were subject to limitations but also in case of the districts selected, there were varying levels of agricultural and institutional development at the time of selection. The basic cropping patterns were different in the various districts owing to their location in different agroclimatic zones. In respect of average size of farms, there were marked differences. Differences also existed in respect of the percentage of irrigation availability as a consequence of which input use varied distinctly. Not only were the situations so widely differing among the selected districts but also the conditions within the districts themselves were not uniform. Practically every IADP district was heterogeneous in its development potential. This fact was given little notice at the beginning of the programme. The extent of the production effort over a heterogeneous area is not often shown by an overall average alone. This has clearly been seen, for example, in the case of West Godavari district where in a year of relatively heavy rainfall higher yields in the upland have wholly or partially been offset by reduced yields in parts of the delta region due to floods or water-logging. Similar is the situation in Raipur, Aligarh, Thanjavur and several other districts.

The review of the IADP inter-district situation brings out clearly that the districts (or areas within districts) which at a distance appeared to be similar, nevertheless were often found on closer examination to vary in many respects in their agricultural resources base, in infrastructure, and in technological base, etc. The overall picture at the beginning of IADP then was not one of 15 carefully selected districts starting from a uniform base line and moving forward to modernisation and higher production. Rather, it was a highly varied picture with some districts already well started on the path and other much further behind with only a bare beginning.

The establishment of IADP was a new dimension in the direction of modernising Indian agriculture. Since the IADP was grafted on the existing programme, despite its several advantages, it suffered from various limitations.

An evaluation report (1966) on the second year of the working of IADP showed that the IADP also failed to bring about coordination. One of the important lessons that one can draw from the implementation of the IADP is that the administrative system is not adequate for the job and has to be geared to the needs of the programme. In fact, one of the most serious obstacles that the IADP has had to face is the archaic administrative system that is prevalent in the country. This system, based essentially on cheques and balances, having evolved in different times and for different purposes, has proved woefully inadequate for any operation the aim of which is not to maintain the status quo but to change it. Tne IADP has thus been a square peg in a round hole.[50]

Another serious flaw in the IADP strategy was the inadequatc attention towards the constraints to the adoption of the new technology faced particularly by the small and marginal farmers. Unless a strategy is evolved to combine the scarce resources of technical, financial and administrative inputs with the managerial inputs of the efficient farmers, rapid growth in agricultural production may no be achieved.[51]

The High-Yielding Varieties Programme

The Mexican Dwarf varieties of wheat developed by the Rockfeller Foundation was first released to Asian farmers in 1965. The IR 8 variety of rice researched at the International Rice Research Institute in Philippines was first made available in 1966. Within a year or two, by 1967-68, the new varieties had been planted in 15 per cent of the wheat acreage in India and Pakistan and about 6 per cent of the rice acreage in India and Philippines with good progress also reported from Afghanistan, Ceylon, Indonesia, Malaysia and Turkey.[52] Since then, in each one of the seasons that followed, adoption rate accelerated. The testimony of the International Rice Research Institute in 1968 has this to say about its sharp spread: "The initial thrust of the new technology has been far more rapid than any previous historical experience. In many areas the level of adoption has exceeded even the most optimistic predictions."[53]

The evolution of high-yielding varieties of seeds marks a turning point in the modernisation of traditional Indian agriculture. The draft outline of the Fourth Plan asserted that it is necessary to make far greater use of modern methods of production and to bridge the gap between demand and production by the application of the latest advance in the science of agriculture.[54] A similar view was expressed by a Government publication in April 1965. It said that the history of economic development in general and agricultural development in particular of other countries of the world shows that transformation of traditional agriculture is possible through strong injection of modern technology and scientific technique on a massive scale.[55]

The New Agricultural Strategy which aimed at a rapid and spectacular increase in foodgrains production was adopted from 1966-67. Although an improved strategy in agricultural development in terms of IADP and IAAP was already working in the country, the fundamental departure in the new agricultural technology was the introduction of intensive cultivation using new high yielding varieties of seeds backed by more and better plant nutrients, effective plant protection and adequate water supply.[56] In the new agricultural strategy, a three-dimensional approach towards agricultural development was adopted which consisted of high yielding variety programmes, adoption of modern chemical technology and foodgrains price support policy.[57] This programme envisaged a super intensive type of agricultural development based on a package of principles involving high factor inputs on new varieties capable of giving very high yields.[58]

Coming to an examination of the performance of the new technology it is found that it has really changed the shape of Indian agriculture. The most remarkable feature of agricultural production during the first three years of the Fifth Plan (1974-79) was the record foodgrains harvest during 1975-76.[59] The output of foodgrains rose to 121.03 million tonnes from a level of 99.8 million tonnes in 1974-75. The output of rice rose by 25 per cent, from 39.6 million tonnes to 48.74 million tonnes. The output of coarse grains increased by nearly 3.8 million tonnes, and that of pulses by a little over 3.1 million tonnes. After registering a sharp increase of 15.2 per cent in the year 1975-76, agricultural production in 1976-77, however, declined by 6.7 per cent. Total foodgrains production was lower by 9.5 million tonnes than the peak of a little over 121 million tonnes reached in the previous year. The production of all foodgrains except jowar and wheat, registered a decline. The output of rice was lower by nearly 6 million tonnes, of maize by 1 million tonnes, of barley by 0.9 million tonnes, and of pulses by a little under 2 million tonnes. The production of jowar, however, increased by 0.9 million tonnes and that of wheat by 0.2 million tonnes.

Agricultural production which had experienced a decline in the previous year registered a significant increase in 1977-78. The output of foodgrains at 125.6 million tonnes was 14.4 million tonnes higher than that in 1976-77 and 4.6 million tonnes more than in 1975-76. Out of the 14.4 million tonnes increase in foodgrains production, rice contributed 10.8 million tonnes, jowar 1.3 million tonnes and wheat 2.3 million tonnes. On the other hand, the production of bajra declined by nearly 20 per cent; maize and barley suffered a small decline and the production of pulses registered only a marginal increase.

The total area under high-yielding variety seed programme increased from 26.02 million hectares in 1973-74 to 34.48 million hectares in 1976-77, an increase of more than 2 million hectares in one year and nearly 7.5 million hectares in two years. The increase took place mainly in rice, wheat and jowar. Simultaneously, the irrigation potential went up in 1976-77 from over 2 million hectares to 47 million hectares. This increase was shared equally by major, medium and minor irrigation schemes. The achievement in respect of fertiliser consumption was even more significant. Total fertiliser consumption in 1976-77 increased to the extent of 3.4 million tonnes as against 2.9 million tonnes in 1975-76 and 2.84 million tonnes in 1973-74.

It can also be seen that despite the initial good impact, the pace of progress in respect of the new technology has been slow in totality with much slower pace in many crops except wheat, where progress was substantial. In productivity too the highest growth rate has been experienced by wheat after 1964-65, where the productivity growth rate of 0.9 per cent during the pre-green revolution rose to 4.6 per cent during the post-green revolution period. Bajra and pulses have also witnessed small gains in productivity but in case of paddy and maize the situation has been different. Paddy productivity experienced a growth rate of 2.1 per cent during the pre-green revolution period but fell to 1.9 per cent during the post green revolution period. Maize experienced a negative growth rate of productivity (—0.1 per cent) during 1964-74 in comparison to productivity growth rate of 3.1 per cent during 1953-63 In order to study the changes in growth rates of output Rao took two periods, viz., 1949-50 to 1959-60 and 1961-62 to 1971-72 and arrived at the conclusion that despite technological changes, the growth rate in the output of foodgrains and of agricultural commodities, as a whole, decelerated during the decade ending 1970-71 compared to the previous decade.[60]

Since the entire benefits of the new technology was reaped by a single crop 'wheat', some of the economists have rightly called this agricultural revolution a 'wheat revolution'. It may be concluded that during the period 1964-65 to 1974-75 which has seen the introduction of high-yielding variety seeds in case of many food crops and mechanisation of agricultural operations, Indian agriculture has virtually witnessed a 'wheat revolution' instead of green revolution.[61] Srinavasan[62] also termed this revolution a 'wheat revolution'.

The high-yielding varieties programme made limited progress with the exception of wheat where the area under this programme rose from 0.54 million hectares in 1966-67 to 15.50 million hectares in 1977-78 and the target at 16.50 million hectares in 1978-79.

Apart from the fact that the new technology led to a limited increase in production and productivity, it also had several harmful distributional effects. It led to the widening of disparities both regional and personal.[63] As pointed out by many, the new technology is dependent upon water. This has led to its adoption in areas with assured irrigation and non-adoption in dry areas. Thus regional inequality is inherent in this innovation. It is also argued that new technology has served the interests of big landlords[64] despite the fact that its application does not necessarily require large sized farms. This scale neutrality has not worked to the advantage of small farmers. Largely because of the institutional set up that is subservient to big landowners or rich farmers,[65] agricultural inputs, chemical fertilisers in particular, were largely cornered by these powerful people. Small-sized farmers handicapped the poor farmers because they were neither well-equipped with resources nor with water supplies. Given the need for complex agricultural techniques and the use of inputs in correct proportion and in time the green revolution tended to be concentrated in the farms of 'big' people normally with large-sized farms. They command resources, get knowledge and extension services as also all those advantages which could facilitate the successful application of the new technique. Fedder,[66] generalising about the experiences of the new technology in underdeveloped countries correctly said, "The green revolution is a programme for large landowners par excellence and cannot be different; they are already better equipped, have almost exclusive access to input and output markets, and are the major, if not the almost exclusive recipients of agricultural credit." As a consequence of the concentration of the new technology on large farms the inequalities have further increased.

This regrettable feature of the new technology that it has bypassed the small farmers, and has become the handmaid of the rich to become more rich, is too obvious to be seen and the reasons are not far to seek. Among them, the following three are the principal ones: One, the new method of cultivation is expensive which the small farmer is not able to meet. Two, the use of this technology presupposes the requisite knowledge about it and a proper application of the same. Three, besides being expensive in terms of money and non-monetary resources the application of this technology is pregnant with risks which small farmers are unable to undertake in the present setup.

In the late sixties some analysts were questioning about the success of the high-yielding varieties programme. For example, the Agricultural Prices Commission had written: "The emergence of the high-yielding varietics of seeds and the receptivity of the cultivators to these seeds does of course represent a qualitative change in the situation but the experience of what has so far been achieved through these varieties calls for a certain caution in projecting the rate of growth of foodgrain output over the next few years—as between different grains and different States their impact has been uneven and overall quite modest."[67]

Ashok Mitra,[68] the Chairman of the Agricultural Prices Commission had written: "At this stage, we can therefore at best hardly afford to slide into romanticisim: the agricultural revolution is still a prospective event. This year's harvest implies a process of recovery from the harrowing two years following 1964-65 but atleast for the present not very much more than that."

Rao[69] also questions the validity of the new technology. He argues: "there are reasons to believe that even without the Green Revolution the growth rate would have been maintained at 2-2.5 per cent per annum." The reasons he adduces are: "The growth of population at about 2.2 per cent per annum has been exerting an upward pressure on prices of agricultural commodities. This would have provided incentives to the farmers for expanding output and would have induced the Government to invest in irrigation, fertilisers, etc."[70] Dantwala's[71] reaction to this explanation of Rao's appears genuine and reasonable. "Apart from the fact that under static technology high prices have little impact on aggregate production, it is surprising that one so deeply concerned with poverty of the Indian masses should wish to rely on high food price path of growth of population instead of welcoming the cost-reducing technology for achieving increased production." Rao maintains that some of the inputs, for example, fertiliser, would have been used at a certain rate even before the advent of the new technology but he was unaware of the fact that application of higher doses of fertilisers to traditional seeds was unremunerative as it did not increase output. Moreover, there is a clear evidence to indicate that the growth in the cropped area was slowing down from 2.1 per cent per annum during 1949-50—1960-61 to 0.6 per cent during 1960-61—1970-71. Under the circumstances, adoption of the new technology was the only solution to the food problem of the country.

Several studies on the impact of new technology on income distribution show that inequality has increased after the adoption of the new technology as compared to that prior to it. Studies by Mishra,[72] Rao,[73] Chowdhry[74] and Rudhra[75] have concluded that the new technology has been more favourable to large farmers than to small and marginal farmers.

A report on 'Technological Advance in Indian Agriculture' by Mellor[76] pointed out that the direct effect of the new agricultural technologies would provide proportionately greater benefits to landowners than to landless labourers; hence the wider existing income disparities. Indirect effects of expanded farm operation mainly through water supply, control and expanded non-farm employment might eventually narrow these gaps.

Since the introduction of the new agricultural technology conflicting views are being expressed regarding its impact on employment in the agricultural sector. Many studies conducted in India and abroad have concluded that rapid adoption of new farm technology is supposed to provide an adequate and continuous employment to the rural population. Since new technology would give rise to multiple cropping and also to greater intensity of cropping, it offers the possibility of absorbing a considerable fraction of the growing labour force into productive employment.[77] Supporting this viewpoint the report of the National Commission on Labour (1969) says:

> "Report from States indicates that the agricultural production programme has resulted in more employment, reduction of under-employment, increase in wages (both in cash and kind) above the minimum wages fixed under the Act, and general improvement in the economic condition of labour."[78]

Ladejinsky[79] observed, "the new technology is characterised by frequent application of water, fertilisers, insecticides, weeding, double cropping, bigger crops, larger volume of transportation, marketing, and food processing. All these are more labour-demanding at primary, secondary and tertiary levels."

Thus, we see that according to this group of researchers new technology is employment-oriented. However, the other school of thought has some pessimistic views about the increasing use of new technology and employment.

A study conducted by Bal[80] reveals that human labour was used to the extent of 905.75 hours per hectare on pure bullock-operated farms and 756.18 hours per hectare on bullock-operated farms owning tube-wells/engines thereby reducing the labour requirement by 16.51 per cent with the first stage of mechanisation. At full mechanisation stage, human labour was used to the extent of 833.33 hours per hectare which when compared with pure bullock farms shows that full mechanisation decreased total human labour employment by 7.87 per cent.

Ladejinsky,[81] in his field trip to Punjab remarks: "talking about Punjab and keeping in mind most of the Northern wheat belt of India, a reversal of the current demand of more employment created by the present stage of new technology is inevitable."

Soltani[82] examined the problem of labour utilisation in three agricultural regions of Fars Province in the South Central Iran. He arrived at the conclusion that "full mechanisation of wheat production results in the displacement of nearly 131 hours of labour per hectare.

Shrivastava, Brown and Heady[83] have examined the effect of a new agricultural strategy on farm employment in their article, 'Green Revolution and Farm Income Distribution'. They concluded: "since mechanisation may dampen the increase in labour demand resulting from the expanding factor of seed fertilisers, the policies that encourage premature mechanisation in surplus labour economies such as India's do not seem conducive to solving the problem of growing unemployment."

From the foregoing discussions it follows that mechanisation in a few cases has also tended to decrease labour employment slightly. However, the work done is too scanty to arrive at a firm conclusion. Reviewing the overall performance of HYVs Programme, it becomes evident that the "growth with equitable distribution" theory received little impetus during this phase and the need for a target-based approach to rural development became imperative.

Target-based Programmes

The programme of modern inputs in intensive areas and the high yielding varieties programme not only quickened the process of economic polarisation in rural areas but also contributed to increasing social antagonisms.[84] The All India Rural Credit Review Committee, set up by the Reserve Bank of India in 1966, to review the supply of rural credit concluded that the various programmes of rural development initiated in the country since 1950-51 have not provided adequate benefits to the small farmers. These groups have also not been able to have sufficient access to institutional credit. Since they occupy a large chunk of the agricultural holdings and are as progressive as the rich farmers, their gross neglect would lead to far-reaching socio-economic implications.[85] It was this conclusion on which the All India Rural Credit Review Committee recommended for setting up of an institution to be called the 'Small Farmers' Development Agency' (SFDA) in certain selected districts. The idea was basically to identify the problems of small farmers as cultivators to suggest ways and means to overcome these problems and to provide adequate facilities to them in the form of agricultural inputs as well as credit. In close collaboration with the Planning Commission the Committee managed to make the recommendation acceptable to the Government. The Fourth Five Year Plan gave an outline of the measures that were to be provided to the small farmers for ameliorating their conditions. These measures apart from minor irrigation, agricultural credit and animal husbandry, included proposals for the construction of community works such as tanks and tubewells for the small farmers. A reorientation of policies on government loans towards small farmers was also envisaged. In addition, specific projects were to be designed for small farmers in about forty-five selected districts, and these were to be implemented by a Small Farmers' Development Agency (SFDA) in each of these districts.

Another section which had been hitherto neglected in planning for rural development was that of the sub-marginal farmers and agricultural labourers. The Fourth Plan expressed equal concern for them and felt that unless large avenues of employment opportunities were provided to them, they would continue languishing in the quagmire of apathy and indifference. Accordingly, forty projects were proposed to be located around urban periphery so that employment-oriented activities such as poultry, dairy-farming etc., could be developed. The schemes were sanctioned in 1970-71 and began to be implemented the following year. For the purpose of administration apart from SFDA, another agency, the Marginal Farmers' and Agricultural Labourers' Agency (MFALA)[86] was set up to work at the district level.

The function of the SFDAs was to quantify the number of small farmers in an area, investigate and identify the nature and extent of their problem, formulate programmes to deal with the problem and devise ways and means of implementing the programme. The functions of the MFAL agencies were to identify genuine marginal farmers and agricultural labourers, identify the nature and assess the magnitude of their problems, formulate economic programmes for providing gainful employment to them, arrange for the procurement of inputs and for the provision of facilities for production, processing, storage and marketing etc.

Whereas the SFDA focussed on projects related to farming like multiple cropping, introduction of HYVs programme, horticulture, development of minor irrigation, soil conservation, land development etc., the MFALA, on the other hand, laid stress on the provision of subsidiary occupations and other employment generating programmes. All the SFDAs and the MFALAs were started as two separate bodies initially. It was in June 1974 that the Government of India decided to merge the two into a single agency.[87] In 1973, the Steering Group on the Fifth Five Year Plan pointed out that the performance of the agencies was highly uneven.[88] The Programme Evaluation Organisation's report on the performance of SFDA and MFALA schemes was also not very encouraging.[89] The greatest pitfall with these schemes was the lack of an effective and efficient administrative machinery.[90] Lack of sufficient credit facilities was also a major constraint on small and marginal farmers in adopting improved agricultural techniques and undertaking economic activities.[91] Other problems with the MFALAs was related to the wrong identification of beneficiaries, complicated and time consuming procedure of giving of subsidies etc. Since the coverage of the SFDAs was limited, its impact on rural life was at best marginal. The SFDAs remained in operation till the end of the Fifth Five Plan and on October 2, 1980 it became a part of the much talked about Integrated Rural Development Programme. Commenting on the performance of the SFDAs and MFALAs, the Sixth Five Year Plan remarked: "It will be seen that while the numbers identified for assistance represented only a segment and not the whole of the target group, the numbers benefited are only about half the numbers identified. Furthermore, the nature of assistance given to the bulk of them comprised items which did not lead to any specific additional asset creation. The actual impact of these items of assistance on the income of beneficiaries, therefore, varied a great deal and in many cases has been of doubtful significance."[92]

Area-based Programmes

Although the target-based programmes did provide some concern for the marginal man,[93] it was realised that in certain areas a mere implementation of the programmes for the weaker section would not suffice to solve the problem of abject poverty. There were certain areas which could not develop owing to the scarcity of rainfall. Nearly one-fifth of India's total land area suffers from varying degrees of scarcity in rainfall and is thus subject to drought.[94] The drought prone areas in the country received Government's attention only before independence.[95] The Britishers showed great concern in the development of such regions. In 1970, the Government of India launched the Rural Works Programme (RWP) to promote the integrated development of areas which were chronically affected by drought to mitigate scarcity conditions in them. The launching of the RWP, however, depended on the identification of the drought prone areas for which the Government set up a committee of experts identifying such areas on the basis of certain objective criteria like the incidence of rainfall over a period of time, extent of irrigation in the area, and the conditions of drought. Thus fifty-four drought prone areas were identified representing seventy-two districts in thirteen States. The RWP was launched in these areas as an employment-oriented programme with special emphasis on labour-intensive employment opportunities like soil conservation, afforestation, road construction, and provision of irrigation facilities. However, the RWP was unable to provide employment avenues on a regular basis. In 1972-73 the RWP was modified and given the name of the Drought Prone Areas Programme (DPAP). The DPAP was originally designed as an employment generation programme but later on its focus shifted to development works so that it could provide a permanent solution to the problem of drought rather than piecemeal solutions to the problem of unemployment. The sole responsibility of administering the DPAP rests with the District Rural Development Agency (DRDA).[96]

A subsidiary to the DPAP was the Desert Development Programme (DDP) launched in 1977-78 in pursuance of the recommendations of the National Commission on Agriculture.[97] The programme aimed at an integrated development of desert areas by increasing the productivity, income level, and employment opportunities of the people through optimum utilisation of physical, human, livestock and other biological resources.[98]

In fact that the administration of the DPAP was entrusted to an agency already engaged in the implementation of various programmes such as the IRDP and NREP, created several problems. The most serious of these was that the DRDA could not naturally provide equal care and attention to a whole set of programmes as a result of which the DPAP got sidetracked. The DPAP or for that matter, the DDP did not have the mass appeal like the anti-poverty programmes of IRDP or NREP. A single machinery entrusted with the implementation of the IRDP/NREP and the DPAP/DDP will sometimes be constrained to make unsound compromises, to say nothing of the neglect that a technology-based programme has to suffer in such circumstances.[99] The implementation processes in the DPAP were also weak and faulty. Many schemes were dropped even after they had been sanctioned. The projects started, unnecessarily extended their periods of gestation and mid-term revisions of schemes led to an unavoidable waste of funds.[100]

Minimum Needs Programme

At this stage of planning, a serious debate was going on in India whether the area approach to rural development would bring about equity in distribution of the gains of development or whether the target approach would offer more fruitful prescriptions for bringing about equality. While the area approach suffered from limitations discussed above, it was being realised that the high-yielding variety seed-fertiliser-pesticide technology was having a very strong impact on the 'growth with inequitable distribution' theory, with clear evidences of a wider demarcation between the assets of the bigger (richer) and the smaller (poorer) farmers. As a supplement to this, much more emphasis had to be given to programmes based on minimum needs. Apart from this, the target approach, as adopted in India catered to the needs of a specific group of people—the small and marginal farmers and agricultural labourers, and not necessarily those whose basic needs remained unfulfilled. In view of the high incidence of poverty, as discussed in the earlier chapter, the need for a programme on the basic minimum needs appeared imperative. According to an ILO report, the satisfaction of basic needs meant meeting the minimum requirements of a family for personal consumption; access to essential services; provision of job to every individual willing to work; satisfaction of needs of a more qualitative nature and popular participation in the making of decisions.[101] Basic needs strategy implies a rise in the incomes of the poverty groups by offering them higher prices for their products and labour service and providing them things at cheaper prices, and by redistributing the existing stock of capital through measures like land reforms.[102] The FAO also observed that an effective strategy for meeting basic needs required not only redistribution with growth, but also a positive shift of resources towards the satisfaction of basic needs as part of the strategy and not merely a secondary consequence of it.[103] Basic needs approach does not necessarily imply sacrificing the objective of accelerating growth. In fact, growth is a necessary concomitant for the satisfaction of basic needs, which in turn necessitates the orientation of growth towards the supply and distribution of essential goods and services.[104] Production of mass consumption goods is mostly based on agro-based industries, which might well be established in rural areas. They are also quite labour intensive.[105] Basic needs strategy is designed to improve the income earning opportunities of the poor and the participation of the poor in the ways in which their needs are met.[106]

Based on the strategy of basic needs, the Minimum Needs Programme (MNP) was thus introduced in India in the Fifth Five Year Plan (1974-79). It was visualised as an investment in human resource development, especially for those who were below the poverty line.[107] The elements of the MNP include elementary education, rural health, rural water supply, rural roads, rural electrification, housing for the landless labourers, etc. The Sixth Plan (1980-85) envisaged a big increase in the minimum needs programme with a total outlay of Rs. 5807 crores against Rs. 2607 crores in the Fifth Plan.[108] Commenting on the success of the basic needs strategy, an ILO report observed that it depends on (i) a package approach, which combines different but interrelated elements; (ii) structural changes and major policy reorientation; (iii) greater access of poverty groups to resources, appropriate fiscal and other policies for resource mobilisation, the redistribution of income and the institutional reforms to translate policies into action; (iv) political commitment and appropriate administrative capacity and structure, and (v) organisation of the rural poor with a view to ensure their participation in the policy making process.[109]

Notes and References

1. Sundaram, I.S., Antipoverty Rural Development in India, D.K. Publications, New Delhi, 1984, p. 20.
2. World Bank, The Assault on World Poverty, John Hopkins University Press, Baltimore, 1975, p. 3.
3. See Dr.V.K.R.V. Rao's paper submitted to the Third Biennial Conference of the Association & Development Research and Training Institutes of Asia and the Pacific, Eastern Economist, Oct. 12, 1977, p. 742. For other definitions of Rural Development, see Mohsin, Nadeem, Rural Development Through Government Programmes, Mittal Publications, New Delhi, 1985. Also see Singh, Tarlok, "Integrated rural development", Kurukshetra, Oct. 1, 1977, p. 14; Anker, Desmond L.W., "Rural development, problems and strategies", International Labour Review, Vol. 108, 1973; Rao, V.K.R.V., Kurukshetra, May 16, 1978, p. 12; Kahlon, A.S., "Integrated rural development: a human resource centred approach", Agricultural Situation in India, April 1979, p. 3.
4. Gaikward, V.R., "Rural development strategies—evaluation of some early experiments in India", in Dantwala, et. al. (ed.), Asian Seminar on Rural Development: The Indian Experience,

Oxford and IBH Publishing Company Private Limited, New Delhi, 1986, p. 17.

5. Ibid., p. 18.
6. Ibid., p. 20.
7. Tagore, Rabindranath, Glimpses of Bengal, MacMillan and Company. 1921.
8. Elmhirst, Leonard, "Rabinath Tagore and Sriniketan", in Evolution of Community Development Programme in India, Government of India, New Delhi, 1963, p. 1.
9. Hatch, Spencer, "Early times at Martandam project", in Evolution of Community Development Programme in India, Government of India, New Delhi, 1973, p. 15.
10. Verma, S.R., "The Gurgaon experiment", in Evolution of Community Development Programme in India, Government of India, New Delhi, 1973, p. 27.
11. Mayer, A. et. al., Pilot Project India, Berkley : University of California Press, 1958, p. 40.
12. Op. cit., (4) p. 20.
13. Op. cit. (7).
14. Nehru, Jawaharlal, The Discovery of India, The Signet Press, Calcutta, 1946, p. 57.
15. Mukerji, D.P., Diversities, Essays in Economics, Sociology and other Social Problems, People's Publishing House, p. 34.
16. Op. cit. (8).
17. Dasgupta, Sugata, "Tagore's experiment in rural reconstruction : a poet and a plan", in History of Rural Development in Modern India, Mittal and Khan (ed.), Vol. IV, Gandhian Institute of Studies, Varanasi, 1976, p. 215.
18. Op. cit. (9), p. 15.
19. Op. cit. (10), p. 27.
20. Ibid., p. 34.
21. Kavoori J.C., "Baroda experiment", in History of Rural Development in Modern India, Mittal and Khan (ed.), Vol. IV, Gandhian Institute of Studies, Varanasi, 1976, p. 190. Also see Desai, I.P. and B. Chawdhary, History of Rural Development in India, Vol. II, Impex India, Delhi, 1977, p. 7, and Krishnamachari, V.T., "Community development in Baroda State", in Evolution of Community Development Programme in India, Government of India, New Delhi, 1973, p. 36.
22. Ibid., p. 192.

23. Desai, I.P. and B. Chawdhary, History of Rural Development in India, Vol. II, Impex India, Delhi, 1977, p. 8.
24. Op. cit. (4), p. 50.
25. Harijan, 19th June, 1937.
26. Gandhi, M.K., Rebuilding Our Villages (ed.) Bharatan Kumarappa, Navajivan Publishing House, Ahmedabad, 1956.
27. Op. cit. (4), p. 60.
28. Op. cit. (11).
29. Kavoori, J.C. and B.N. Singh, History of Rural Development in Modern India, Vol. I, Impex India, New Delhi, 1967, p. 125.
30. See the report of the 'Grow More Food Enquiry Committee', Government of India, p. 53.
31. In compliance with Operational Agreement No. 8 signed on 31st May, 1952, the U.S. Government made available to the Government of India, the necessary finance, equipment, material and technical personnel for starting approximately 55 projects on rural development located in selected areas in several States of the country—excerpts from Community Projects : a draft.
32. Krishnamachari, V.T., Community Development, Government of India, Chapter I, p. 2.
33. Taylor, Carl C., "Community development programme and methods", Community Development Review, Dec. 1956, in Chaudhari T.P.S. (ed.), Selected Readings in Community Development, National Institute of Community Development, Hyderabad, 1967, p. 7.
34. Mukerji, B., Community Development in India, Orient Longman, Calcutta, 1967, p. 1. Also see Taylor, Carl C., India's Roots of Democracy: A Sociological Analysis of Rural India's Experiences in Planned Development Since Independence, Orient Longman, Calcutta, 1967, p. 609.
35. U.N. Report on Community Development Progress in India, Pakistan and Philippines, 1955.
36. The First Five Year Plan, Planning Commission, Government of India, p. 223.
37. Poston, R.W., Democracy Speaks Many Tongues, New York, 1959, p. 16.
38. Agarwal, A.N., Indian Agriculture: Problem, Progress and Prospects Vikas Publishing House, New Delhi, 1980.

39. Evolution of Community Development Programme in India, Ministry of Community Development and Cooperation, Government of India, 1965, p. 44.
40. Tangri, P.P., "India's Community Development Programme: Critique and suggestion, in Hambidge Gove (ed.), Dynamics of Development, Universal Book Stall, Delhi, 1967, p. 311.
41. Misra, R.P. et. al., Regional Development Planning in India, Vikas Publishing Company, New Delhi, 1976, p. 143.
42. Sen, L.K. et.al., People's Image of Community Development and Panchayati Raj, National Institute of Community Development, Hyderabad, 1969, p. 28.
43. Danda, Ajit K., "Rural reconstruction: an Indian experience, in Ajit K. Danda (ed.), Studies on Rural Development, Inter India Publications, New Delhi, 1984, p. 10.
44. Ibid., p. 11.
45. Jain, L.C., et. al., Grass without Roots: Rural Development Under Government Auspices, Sage Publications, New Delhi, 1985, p. 38.
46. Sadhu, A.N. and Amarjit Singh, New Agricultural Strategy: Its Implications, Marwah Publications, New Delhi, 1980, p. 16.
47. The Third Five Year Plan, Planning Commission, Government of India, 1961, p. 316.
48. Ibid.
49. Op. cit. (46), p. 25.
50. Second report of the Expert Committee of Assessment and Evaluation of IADP, Ministry of Food and Agriculture, Government of India, 1966.
51. Desai, D.K., "Intensive Agricultural District Programme: analysis of the results", Economic and Political Weekly, (Review of Agriculture), June 1969, p. A-90. Few researchers are of the opinion that IADP would have had a greater impact had it been implemented in some of the backward districts. See, for instance, Mohan, Rakesh and Robert E. Evenson, "The Intensive Agricultural District Programme: a new evaluation", Journal of Development Studies, April 1975, p. 135.
52. World Bank Annual Report, 1968, Washington, Reprinted in G. Meier (ed.), Leading Issues in Economic Development, Oxford University Press, 1975, p. 452.
53. International Rice Research Institute, Annual Report 1968, quoted in M.L. Dantwala, "From Stagnation to Growth" in Charan D. Wadhwa, Some Problems of India's Economic Policy, Tata McGraw Hill, New Delhi, 1977, pp. 5 to 9.

54. Op. cit. (23), p. 175.
55. Agricultural Development: Problem and Perspective, Department of Agriculture, Government of India, April 1965, p. 3.
56. I.C.A.R., A New Strategy in Agriculture, (a collection of the speeches by C. Subramaniam), 1972, p. 40.
57. Sen, Sudhir, A Richer Harvest, New Horizons for Developing Countries, McGraw Hill, New Delhi, 1974, p. 196.
58. Robertson, C.A. and R.K. Sharma, "Lessons from the package programme with implications for new agricultural strategy", Indian Journal of Agril. Economics, Vol. XXI, Oct.-Dec. 1966, p. 123.
59. Economic Survey, 1977-78.
60. Rao, C.H.H., Technological Change and Distribution of Gains in Indian Agriculture, MacMillan, Delhi, 1975, p. 11.
61. Op. cit. (46), p. 45.
62. Op. cit. (38), p. 327.
63. Ibid.
64. Griffin, Keith, Political Economy of Agrarian Change: An Essay on the Green Revolution, MacMillan, London, 1974.
65. Ibid.
66. Fedder, E., "The peasant's perspectives in underdeveloped countries", Monthly Review, New York, May 1975, p. 22.
67. Government of India, Report of the Agricultural Prices Commission on Price Policy for Kharif Cereals for 1968-69 Season, Ministry of Food, Agriculture, Community Development and Co-operation, (Department of Food), New Delhi, Sept. 1968, p. 4.
68. Mitra, Ashok, "Bumper harvest has created some dangerous illusions", The Statesman, Oct. 14-15. 1968.
69. Dantwala, M.L., "Agricultural policy in India since independence", Indian Journal of Agril. Economics, No. 4, Oct.-Dec. 1976, p. 43.
70. Ibid.
71. Ibid.
72. Mishra, G.P., "The green revolution: changes and challenges", Eastern Economist, September 1973.
73. Rao, C.H.H., "Farm size and credit policy", Economic and Political Weekly, Dec. 26, 1970.
74. Chowdhry, B.K., "Disparity in income in the context of H.Y.V.", Economic and Political Weekly, Sept. 26, 1970.
75. Rudhra, A., "Big farmers in Punjab", Economic and Political Weekly, Dec. 27, 1969.

76. Mellor, J.W., Report on "Technological advance in Indian agriculture, as it relates to the distribution of income", Dec. 12, 1969.

77. Johnston, B.F. and John Cownie, "Seed, fertiliser revolution", American Economic Review, September, 1969.

78. Report of the National Commission on Labour, 1969, p. 407.

79. Ladejinsky, Wolf, "How green is the green revolution", Economic and Political Weekly, Review of Agriculture, Dec. 1973, p. A-77.

80. Bal, H.S., "Impact of mechanisation of farm labour employment", Agricultural Situation in India, Sept. 1974, p. 385.

82. Soltani, G.R., "The effects of farm mechanisation on labour utilisation and its social implications, Indian Journal of Agricultural Economics, Vol. XXIX, No. 1, Jan.-March, 1974.

83. Shrivastava, U.K. et.al., "Green revolution and farm income distribution", Economic and Political Weekly, Review of Agriculture, Dec. 1971, p. A-171.

84. Jain, S.C., Rural Development, Institutions and Strategies, Rawat Publications, Jaipur, 1985, p. 24.

85. Report of the all India Rural Credit Review Committee, Reserve Bank of India, Bombay, 1969.

86. Immediately after the schemes under the MFAL agencies were sanctioned by the Government, the Fourth Five Year Plan changed the term 'submarginal' into 'marginal.'

87. The decision was taken vide letter no. 1101/2/74 A.C., dated June 5, 1974, issued by the Ministry of Agriculture and Irrigation, Department of Rural Development, Government of India.

88. For details see the Report of the Steering Group relating to agriculture, irrigation and allied sectors, Fifth Five Year Plan, Planning Commission, Government of India, New Delhi, 1973.

89. The Planning Commission asked its Programme Evaluation Organisation to undertake an evaluation of the schemes of SFDA and MFALA in 1973, This report was finalised in 1979.

90. Ibid.

91. Maheshwari, S., Rural Development in India: A Public Policy Approach, Sage Publications, New Delhi, 1985, p. 97.

92. The Sixth Five Year Plan, Planning Commission, Government of India, New Delhi, p. 168.

93. Op. cit. (91), p. 85.

94. Ibid., p. 100.

95. Ibid., p. 101.

96. The DRDA got its name after the amalgamation of the SFDA and the MFALA, and became the pivot around which the programmes like IRDP, NREP revolved.
97. For details, see the Report of the National Commission on Agriculture, Government of India. The DDP is being implemented in the hot arid deserts comprising eleven districts of Rajasthan, four districts of Haryana and three districts of Gujarat and the cold arid deserts in the Ladakh region of Jammu and Kashmir and the Spiti subdivision of the Lahaul-Spiti district of Himachal Pradesh.
98. Op. cit. (91), p. 110.
99. For details, see the Report of the Task Force on the Drought Prone Areas Programme and the Desert Development Programme, Ministry of Rural Development, Government of India, New Delhi, 1982, p. 29.
100. See the Supplementary Report of the Comptroller and Auditor-General of India for the year 1973-74 (Part I), Comptroller and Auditor General of India, New Delhi.
101. International Labour Organisation, Employment, Growth and Basic Needs: One World Problem, ILO, Geneva, 1976, p. 7.
102. Ibid., p. 34.
103. FAO, "Review and analysis of agrarian reform and rural development in the developing countries since the mid-sixties", undated, p. 125.
104. Lisk, Franklyn, "Conventional development strategies and basic needs fulfilment: a reassessment of objectives and policies", International Labour Review, March-April 1977, p. 187.
105. Haksar, P.N., "Disparity in levels of living", Eastern Economist, August 18, 1972, p. 302.
106. Streeten Paul, "From growth to basic needs", Finance and Development, Sept. 1979, p. 29.
107. Op. cit. (84), p. 38.
108. Sixth Five Year Plan, (1980-85), Planning Commission, Government of India, 1981, p. 223.
109. Op. cit. (101), p. 7.

3

Integrated Rural Development

Nearly three decades of sustained and continuous efforts made India realise that there was something special that was needed to bring it out of the fetters of abject poverty. It had become quite evident that distribution and growth did not go hand in hand, ceteris paribus. The Community Development Programme ended like a cart with broken wheels, although it too was committed to integrated development. Other programmes of rural development accentuated inequality. Even the programmes for the small and marginal farmers as well as for agricultural labourers addressed themselves to two categories and were restricted in their activities. By this time India got enough opportunities to learn from its past mistakes, and it strongly felt the necessity of formulating a strategy based on clientele-specific programmes.[1] Such programmes, as is common knowledge, have spill-over effects and require to be viewed in an integrated perspective. It was also realised that such action-oriented, target-based programmes would for once awaken the bureaucracy from the deep slumber, because more than often the bureaucracy has turned a deaf ear to the cries from the countryside.

The IRDP can be considered to be a modification of the SFD and the MFALD programmes; in fact, a shade better, concentrating its entire energies to the uplift of the rural poor. The fact that it involved science and technology in its application is also praiseworthy. Science and technology led to enormous increases both in production and productivity in the agricultural sector during the late sixties, but its application then could not be exploited to the optimum level, or its full potential for rural transformation still needs to be explored.[3] When Myrdal talked of institutional reforms, Gandhi referred to the provision of man's basic needs through generation of full employment and decentralisation[4], or Schumacher discussed the concept of appropriate technology[5], they all made a reference to the process of integrated development through the application of science and technology in the rural areas.

It was the culmination of ideas of these philosophers and philanthropists and above all the failure on the rural front to alleviate poverty, that led the planners in India to set up a new Department of Science and Technology in 1971. Besides, the election of 1971 was fought on the plank of 'Garibi Hatao' (get rid of poverty), and the Congress Party under Indira Gandhi was firm and resolute in its bid to do justice to the slogan. In 1975, for the first time the Indian Science Congress decided to discuss a cross-disciplinary theme and selected 'Science and Integrated Rural Development' for discussion at its forthcoming session. While addressing the next session of the Indian Science Congress at Waltair the following year, Indira Gandhi vehemently advocated for the application of science for rural development. While delivering the presidential address at the Waltair session, M.S. Swaminathan, the then Director-General of the Indian Council of Agricultural Research, impressed upon Indian scientists the need to integrate science with the task of rural development and even presented a comprehensive plan of action for rural development through the involvement of academic and scientific institutions.

While the seeds of integration in rural development had been implanted in India, internationally too, the concept of integrated rural development was getting wide recognition. The World Bank announced a shift in its lending policy in

1973 in favour of schemes directly benefiting the poor groups in rural areas, with the single objective of alleviating poverty among the rural masses. Even other international organisations and donor agencies pledged themselves to this new strategy of rural development, following the World Bank's move. This offer by the World Bank was plumped with alacrity by Indian planners, who came in the shoes of Pakistan, Bangladesh and a few other countries already implementing the programmes of integrated rural development.

In 1976, Shri C. Subramaniam, the then Finance Minister submitted a blue print on Integrated Rural Development to the House of Parliament which created furore in the Parliament. Nevertheless, it could not make headway owing to the destabilisation in the Congress rule, which ultimately went out of power the following year. Since the Janata Government needed time to settle, the idea of Integrated Rural Development remained merely on paper. It was almost the end of 1980 that saw the crystallisation of the concept of Integrated Rural Development, which laid emphasis on the 'malady-remedy' approach to rural development, making a judicious application of science and technology for the removal of poverty and for people's participation in the programmes of rural reconstruction.[6]

The Concept of Integrated Rural Development

The term 'integration' implies active participation of the development agencies in the programme within a well-planned framework of development for an area. It does not merely refer to the coordination or the extent of cooperation between different departments. It is the integration of all the developmental programmes within an area in consonance with objectives laid down for development by the authorities, the agencies and the people of the area. Integration would therefore imply elimination of all conflicts in the objectives of different participants of development.

Integration, in the Indian context, can be perceived to have three different forms:

1. Functional integration, which refers to the integration of projects with the people in an area. The area development programmes like the DPAP were conceived within this framework. The development of particular area was planned to facilitate the flow of the benefits of special programmes to the people in particular areas.

2. Spatial integration, which refers to the development of urban and rural areas simultaneously with a view to maintaining the rural-urban continuum and facilitate easy flow of resources between the two.

3. Hierarchical integration, which refers to the linking of planning processes at different levels—the Centre, the State, the Block and the village. This type of integration, which is a prerequisite for realistic planning is only possible within a decentralised planning process. It also ensures a two-way linkage in planning.

The concept of integration in rural development was primarily given importance owing to the failure of earlier rural development programmes, and it was realised that in order to confer benefits on the poor, the development strategy should take note of inter-dependence of sectors and proper coordination among various agencies serving the rural poor.[7] Experience has shown that uncoordinated efforts by a multiplicity of agencies do not produce the desired results. The goal of rural development designed to minimise rural poverty can be achieved to a satisfactory extent only through a multidisciplinary apparatus at the local level.[8]

The concept of integration dates back to the fifties when the Government of Maharashtra sanctioned a pilot project named 'integrated area development scheme'. This project was prepared by V.S. Page in 1956 with the idea of improving the lot of small farmers. The scheme, however, could not succeed owing to the following problems:[9]

(i) the various needs of individual cultivators were not properly assessed;

(ii) no attempt was made to concentrate the required inputs on a household in order to ensure economic viability;

(iii) programmes were scattered all over the taluks (blocks), depriving individual cultivators getting any benefit simultaneously from more than one scheme;

(iv) simple schemes were emphasized with no stress on integration or coordination at the district level;

(v) funds allotted were not fully utilised and certain schemes remained incomplete; and

(vi) rich farmers appropriated the maximum benefits of these schemes.

In October 1971, the Planning Commission set up a task force on Integrated Rural Development under the chairmanship of Dr. B.S. Minhas. The interim report submitted the following year, studied the problems of command areas of river valley projects and felt that farm output can be greatly stepped up through better utilisation of local land water resources, supply of adequate inputs and improvement of human skills.[10] It felt that one reason for not using the full potential was lack of coordination between various field functionaries, resulting in overlapping of financial and organisational resources.[11]

Around the mid-seventies, the Council of Scientific and Industrial Research implemented 100 schemes towards integrated rural development in Karim Nagar in Andhra Pradesh. The objective was to bring about changes in the life standards of the poor people of the district through an integrated effort. One very serious lacuna in the programme was its under-emphasis on building and construction programmes, to the neglect of providing gainful employment to the people. The scheme should have concentrated on appropriate technology and shorter gestation projects.[12] Area planning requires a group approach to development in activities related to financing management, marketing and processing. In the absence of this, the project failed to produce any impact on the regional economy.[13]

The concept of integrated rural development has acquired a distinct connotation in economic literature.[14] The term integration has much broader implications than the spatial and functional linkages referred to in the literature in regional economics.[15] Integrated rural development is an aggregative approach to rural problems both in method as well as in content.[16] It is integrative because it extends the social services to the rural people in a combined and cohesive form to achieve balanced development.[17] Integrated rural development means a situation wherein two or more agencies agree upon and work for common goals. These goals have to be approved by participants (and not merely by the agencies) who should have a chance to share in local divisions.[18]

Integrated rural development, according to Subramanyam is the "systematic, scientific and integrated use of all our natural resources and as part of this process enabling every person to engage himself in a productive and socially useful occupation and earn an income that would meet atleast the basic needs."[19] In such a view, the following elements could be identified and considered essential for integrated rural development:[20]

(i) There should be an application of science and technology for the use of natural resources.

(ii) There should be functional linkages between the use of these resources.

(iii) The better use of natural resources should be socially useful and should lead to full employment.

(iv) It should serve the basic needs of society and science and technology should be geared to the production of these.

According to Arora, the concept of integrated rural development needs to incorporate the following elements:[21]

1. Integration of all developmental activities including social services and infrastructure within an area, because such integration will have a mutually reinforcing effect on the rural economy.
2. Focussing of attention on the asset base of the poorest through individual beneficiary schemes.
3. Differential system of subsidy related to the social and financial status of the beneficiary.
4. Attainment of full employment in the operational area by optimum utilisation of resources.
5. People's participation through Panchayati Raj and through people's representatives both at the planning and implementation stages.

While Arora's definition refers to people's participation as an ingredient of integrated rural development, perhaps the gist of his definition lies in the emphasis given to the integration of developmental activities. There is no denying the fact that such a form of integration is the crux of integrated rural development.

Anker defines integrated rural development as the "strategies, policies and programmes for the development of rural areas and the promotion of activities carried out in such areas (agriculture, forestry, fishery, rural crafts and industries, the building of the social and economic infrastructure) with the ultimate aim of achieving a fuller utilisation of available physical and human resources, and thus higher incomes and better living conditions for the rural population as a whole, particularly the rural poor, and effective participation of the latter in the development process."[22]

The idea of integration is also corroborated by Anker. The objective of this integration as discussed by Anker is to improve the living conditions of the poorer groups in rural areas. Anker too, like Arora places emphasis on people's participation as an essential component of rural development.

The brief review of the concept of integrated rural development makes it clear that the application of science and technology for better utilisation of resources is a necessary concomitant for integrated rural development. All these of course have to be geared to the basic needs of rural masses. The process of their use must generate full employment and growth impulses which are retained in the region by area planning which ensures forward and backward linkages.[23] The concept of backward and forward linkages has been discussed by Mohsin.[24] To ensure maintenance of backward linkages, there should be an assurance of the adequate and timely provision of all those inputs which go into the production of an optimum output. For example, if the inputs used were labour time (L), skill of the labourer (Z) and working capital (K), then the resultant output (O) would be,

$$O=f(L, K, Z).$$

Similarly, to ensure the maintenance of forward linkages, there should be a guarantee that the output produced results in the generation of an income adequate enough to raise the beneficiary above the poverty line and at the same time enable him to repay his loan. In this case, income (Y) would be a function of the best price that could be available or,

$$Y=f(p)\ldots \qquad (i)$$

but here price in itself would depend upon the transportation cost (T), marketing facilities (M) and the total output produced (O),

or, $$p=f(T, M, O)\ldots \qquad (ii)$$

Substituting (i) for (ii) we have,

$$Y=f(T, M, O)$$

Strategy for Integrated Rural Development

The strategy of integrated rural development flows from the basic concept of integration and the objective of alleviating rural poverty. This requires a greater flow of resources into the rural areas and a host of interrelated activities discussed below:[25]

1. Shift in terms of trade in favour of the rural people.
2. Resource allocation in favour of rural-centred production activity, like agriculture, household industry, small-scale industries, etc. This can come about through:
   (a) appropriate intervention in the credit market,
   (b) greater allocation of public investment to rural-centred activity,
   (c) an appropriate industrial location policy.
3. A system of quotas and reservations for the poor in order to protect them from market competition.
4. Application of science and technology geared to the production needs of small units.
5. Redistribution of land in favour of the poor in rural areas.
6. Exploitation of surplus labour for the purpose of resource development.

The strategy of rural development with a shift in terms of trade in favour of agriculture is favoured primarily to ensure that the agricultural sector does not suffer in its transactions with the industrial sector. However, the extent of the shift depends upon the character of rural society. If a large proportion of rural households is in the ranks of rural proletariat depending upon the market, and marketed surplus is concentrated in a minority of rural households, the equity effects of such a shift in terms of trade are questionable.[26] Its effects on rural resource development are conditioned by a number of factors like elasticity of input supplies, development of infrastructure, technology, etc.

Rural-centred production activity like agriculture, household industry and small scale industries, etc., have relatively less access to institutional finance and pay higher rates of interests both for fixed and working capital in the private markets. In fact for a long period in the history of commercial banking in rural areas, rural deposits exceeded rural advances suggesting a flow of rural financial resources to the urban centres. Investments of public institutions like state finance corporations and life insurance companies had also a bias towards large industries and within large industries the enterprises of the monopoly groups. The flow of institutional finance to small farms in particular depends upon the strength and viability of the cooperative institutions. While there has been a quantitative expansion of cooperatives in rural areas, they have not primarily been able to deliver the goods. Together with the question of 'urban bias' comes the problem of 'class bias', an issue raised seriously by Griffin, who firmly believes that many policies have often a pronounced class bias which cuts across the sectors or geographical areas of the economy.[27]

It is for this reason that besides public investments in supporting infrastructure for rural production units, investment in cost-reducing technology, quotas and reservations are pleaded for. The operation of quotas and reservations calls for higher levels of efficiency and honesty in administration to enact effective barriers between the two so as to prevent the flow of physical and financial resources intended for the small to the large.[28] Past experience with regard to operation of quotas and reservations has been that a large number of brokers emerge and the flows from the target sector to the non-target sectors are achieved through a variety of manipulations raising the cost structure for the whole economy than what it would be in the absence of quotas and reservations. Socialisation of large enterprises in the consumer goods sector, along with a movement for influencing the want creating mechanism of the market in favour of rural enterprises are necessary even for effective implementation of reservation and quotas and to prevent leakages of resource flows from the target groups in the household and small scale sector to the large scale sector.[29]

Schumacher's concept of appropriate technology[30] provides ample evidence as to how science and technology can be geared to the production needs of small units. Gandhi[31] has also shown the way for the application of science and technology for the benefit of the rural poor. Griffin has discussed at length the effectiveness of land reforms as a measure to eradicate poverty.[32] Exploitation of surplus labour, as practised in China, will go a long way in expediting the process of development.

Notes and References

1. Maheshwari, S.R., Rural Development in India, Sage Publications, New Delhi, 1985, p. 112.
2. Ibid., p. 113.
3. Myrdal, Gunnar, An Approach to the Asian Drama,Vintage Books, 1970.
4. For an excellent review of Gandhian social philosophy, see B.N. Ganguli's Gandhian Social Philosophy.
5. Schumacher, E.F., Small is Beautiful, Harper and Row Publishers, New York, 1973.
6. Arora, R.C., Integrated Rural Development, S. Chand and Company Limited, New Delhi, 1986, p. 4.
7. Sundaram, I.S., Antipoverty Rural Development in India, D.K. Publications, 1984, p. 39.
8. Sixth Five Year Plan, (1980-85), Planning Commission, Government of India, A framework, p. 14.
9. Gaikwad, V.R., Small Farmers: State Policy and Programme Implementation, National Institute of Community Development, Hyderabad, 1971, p. 59.
10. Op. cit. (7), p. 40.
11. Arora, R.C., Development of Agriculture and Allied Sectors: An Integrated Area Approach, S. Chand and Company, New Delhi, p. 4.
12. Op. cit. (7), p. 41.
13. See the article, "Karimnagar: magic, miracle or simply talk of the town", in the Eastern Economist, dated Feb. 25, 1977, p. 340.

14. Parthasarthy, G., "Integrated rural development: concept, theoretical base and contradiction", in D.B. Gupta et. al. (ed.), Development Planning and Policy, Wiley Eastern Limited, New Delhi, 1982, p. 96.

15. Ibid., p. 96.

16. Op. cit. (7), p. 41.

17. See the report on Expert Consultations on Policies and Institutions for Integrated Rural Development, Vol. II, p. 23.

18. East-West Centre, Hawaii, Integrated Communication: Bringing People and Rural Development Together, 1975, p. 12.

19. Subramanyam, C., "Strategy for integrated rural development", Community Development and Panchayati Raj Digest, Vol. 8, April 1977.

20. Op. cit. (14), p. 96.

21. Op. cit. (6), p. 5.

22. Desmond, L.W. Anker, "Rural development: problems and strategies", International Labour Review, Vol. 108, 1973.

23. Parthasarthy, G., "Integrated rural development: concept, theoretical base and contradiction", in T. Mathew ed., Rural Development in India, Agricole Publishing Academy, 1981, p. 27.

24. Mohsin, Nadeem, "Regional rural banks and IRDP", Yojana, July 16-31, 1987, p. 13.

25. Op. cit. (23), p. 34.

26. Ibid., p. 35.

27. Griffin, Keith, Land Concentration and Rural Poverty, Macmillan Publishing Company, 1976.

28. Op. cit. (23), p. 37.

29. Ibid.

30. Op. cit. (5)

31. Op. cit. (4)

32. Op. cit. (27).

4

IRDP: Review of Earlier Studies

The Integrated Rural Development Programme (IRDP) launched in 1978-79 is today a major poverty alleviation programme in the overall strategy of rural development. The main objective of the programme is to transfer productive assets leading to an enlarged resource base of the poorest rural families. The approach relies on transfer of assets and resources to identified households below the poverty line. The transfer is visualised as part of a discreet production programme and not limited to a handing over of certain assets or means of production and income.[1] As an anti-poverty intervention strategy the programme was extended to all the development blocks in the country from Oct. 2, 1980.[2] In the Sixth Five Year Plan, the programme was expected to provide assistance to 15 million families below the poverty line.[3] The capital cost of assets transferred was subsidised to the extent of 25 per cent for small farmers, 33.3 per cent for marginal farmers, agricultural labourers and rural artisans, and 50 per cent for tribal beneficiaries.[4] During 1980-85, the programme covered 165.6 lakh beneficiaries with a total expenditure of approximately Rs. 1,661 crores. The total investment mobilised is reported to be Rs. 4,762.8 crores.[5]

During the Seventh Five Year Plan, poverty still continues to be the most important problem confronting the country and the removal of poverty by the end of the century has been stated as a national goal. In this context, it would be wise to make a quick review of the earlier evaluation studies on IRDP, the single most effective (at least claimbed to be) poverty alleviation programme of the country.

The first and foremost appraisal of IRDP was undertaken by Rath.[6] The main theme of the paper that the IRDP approach, which is based on the distribution of assets to the poor creating self-employment, is not going to deliver the goods and that creation of massive wage employment, both private and public, should be a major strategy for poverty eradication appears to be attractive.[7] Hirway points out that the major grounds on which Rath criticises IRDP can be briefly described as follows:

(1) IRDP is not an integrated programme in the real sense of the term. That is, it does not integrate resource-based or sectoral planning with household-based planning. IRDP is merely a household-based plan whose central attention is on the identification of the rural poor and preparing a plan for these individual beneficiaries.

(2) The Antyodaya approach of IRDP which aims at giving self-employment to the poorest households of the rural society is not a realistic approach as these households are the least capable of taking up self-employment. Most of these households are of the aged and the handicapped or of the poor who have little enterprise or risk-bearing capacity. Studies on IRDP also have shown that these households have fared the worst in various schemes.[8]

(3) The subsidy element of IRDP has encouraged corruption in rural areas and has raised indebtedness of the poor in many cases.

(4) Gains of IRDP have not percolated to the lowest levels. Quoting from the NABARD study, Rath

points out that hardly 18.7 per cent of the total beneficiaries have crossed the poverty line.[9]

(5) The economy does not have enough productive assets for distribution to the poor under IRDP. Consequently, many times assets with very low productivity are given to the poor under the programme. This not only does not help the poor, but it positively harms them.

Rath therefore concludes that the IRDP strategy is largely misconceived. It is capable of helping only a very small number. He argues that putting more burden on this approach will discredit the line of attack, generate wastage, corruption and ultimately cynicism.[10] Though in a multi-pronged attack on rural poverty, this approach has a legitimate place, it cannot be the mainstay of such a programme. According to Rath, the strategy of massive wage-employment generation alone can be the mainstay of the programme.

Hirway argues that Rath's opinion of massive wage employment through IRDP is questionable.[11] According to the 32nd round of the National Sample Survey, 62.52 per cent of the rural working force in India is self-employed in agricultural and non-agricultural sectors put together.[12] This implies that self-employment is a major form of employment in rural India and the family unit is the most common production unit. Will it be realistic then, to base the rural development programmes on wage employment? It seems that even if one wants to change the form of production from family to non-family, it will not be desirable to ignore the needs of the self-employed or of the family units, as such a process will take a long time. Whether we like it or not, self-employment is going to be a major form of employment in our economy for atleast some time to come. It appears that Rath ignores the needs of the self-employed by over-emphasizing wage employment.

In this context, it will be desirable to distinguish between two categories of poor:

(1) those who have atleast some asset or some skill, education or enterprise to take up self-employment, and

(2) those who neither possess any asset nor have any skill, enterprise, education, etc. to take up any activity independently. The former category is likely to get credit from banks while the latter category may not be considered credit-worthy by them. It seems that the poor belonging to the former category should be given assets for self-employment and the latter should be offered wage employment. In other words, the two categories of poor should be treated separately by suitable policy measures.[13]

Unfortunately IRDP clubs both the categories in one and expects even the second category to take up self-employment. IRDP thus over emphasises self-employment as a measure for poverty eradication. Thus, it appears that Rath under-emphasises the needs of unskilled rural labour. If over-emphasis on self-employment is unacceptable, over-emphasis on wage employment also is equally unacceptable. The issue, however, cannot be resolved here as there are serious problems in the working of IRDP. As Rath points out, the gains of IRDP do not percolate to the lower levels in the present socio-economic structure of our rural society.[14] In fact, IRDP feeds corruption on a large scale which benefits mainly the rural elite.[15] The problems of non-percolation and corruption are indeed serious ones which originate from our socio-economic structure.[16] And as long as the desired structural changes are not brought about, it will be difficult to avoid these problems. This also means that rural development should aim at gradual progress in the direction of structural changes. In other words, in the present situation IRDP will bread corruption. But the relevant question here is are we sure that wage-employment programmes will not breed corruption? Corruption on public works programmes has been observed by a number of studies.[17] Misuse of materials, use of substandard materials, paying less than stipulated wages, preparing wrong muster rolls, etc., are reported frequently by these studies. It is also noticed that decisions about NREP works are taken by political leaders without giving any consideration to the extent of poverty and unemployment prevailing in various areas.[18] Corruption is in our system and unless suitable measures are taken, it will be there in all the programmes that we undertake, including NREP and IRDP.

One can say that the question is not whether IRDP can eradicate poverty or whether NREP can do it, but as to how to use both the programmes and sectoral planning in an integrated fashion so that the various needs of the poor are satisfied and the overall goals of rural development are achieved systematically.

Subbarao has done a meticulous review exercise based on three field work based evaluations on IRDP with an all India coverage.[19] According to him, these are the most comprehensive evaluations that have appeared to date. The NABARD study is based on sample households drawn from all over the country.[20] Similar is the case with the PEO study.[21] The IFMR study, however, is confined to five districts from Maharashtra and Tamil Nadu.[22] Though more restricted geographically, IMFR study is based on a much larger sampling fraction than NABARD and PEO studies and includes both beneficiaries and non-beneficiaries.

Both NABARD and PEO studies were carried out during 1983-84 after allowing about two years' time since the inception of the programme in 1980-81. However, Subbarao stresses that the reference year (1982-83) of both these studies was a drought year, and as such the results of both these studies need to be interpreted with caution because the average income from activities such as animal husbandry would have been somewhat depressed due to drought conditions resulting in a sharp escalation of fodder prices in many parts of the country.[23] IMFR study examines the position till February 1982, thus excluding the drought conditions of 1982-83

Referring to the methodological flaws in the three studies, Subbarao observes that the classification adopted by the PEO study for purposes of selection of states poses problems in the interpretation of findings because of overlapping of some of the different seven situations. According to the PEO study the states/districts have been classified into seven different categories,[24] namely:

(a) tribal areas;
(b) hill areas;
(c) agriculturally developed areas;
(d) agriculturally less developed areas;
(e) desert areas;
(f) areas with good administrative infrastructure and
(g) areas with poor administrative infrastructure.

A district with poor administrative infrastructure such as Sultanpur or Mirzapur is also an agriculturally backward region. One wonders whether this categorisation helps or hinders in drawing inferences

Another methodological flaw in all the three studies stems from the fact that they all adopt a before and after approach. Whenever this approach is adopted, it is difficult to know the extent of growth/change caused by factors other than IRDP intervention. For this purpose, it is extremely important to include a control group of non-beneficiary households with similar characteristic in order to make comparisons with beneficiary households. Such a control group was provided for only in IFMR study, but not in NABARD and PEO studies.

In brief, the smallness of the sample, the choice of a drought year to be a reference closing year, and the absence of control group, undoubtedly constitute serious shortcomings of NABARD and PEO studies, and this should be borne in mind before relying (uncritically) on their findings. By contrast, the IFMR study is methodologically superior, but this study allows for only fifteen months after the inception of the programme: an admittedly short period for the benefits to percolate.

Some of the broad findings of the three studies have been indicated by Subbarao. The studies point out that in most cases an indvidual was adopted as a unit of assistance, instead of a family as originally conceived in the programme. The overall effectiveness of the programme was reduced owing to the adoption of a uniform strategy throughout the country with over-emphasis on one or two programmes, disregarding the differences in the level of infrastructural development and institutional structures and in the incidence of poverty. Inflexibility of the programme, standardisation of operations, schematic budgets and uniform procedures for allocation of funds block-wise and scheme-wise, not only reduced the scope of local level initiative, but also did not allow any consideration for regional differences. In addition, the programme funding violated regional equity and has no relationship with the incidence of rural poverty.[25]

With regard to specific findings in programme implementation in different states, the studies highlight the following:

(1) Wrong identification of the beneficiaries is one of the major failings of the programme. The all India average of 16-20 per cent who found their way into the programme is misleading, because there are substantial regional differences. This proportion is as low as 7 per cent in Andhra Pradesh but as high as 47 per cent in Gujarat, according to the NABARD study. The PEO study reveals an unexpected finding: the proportion of non-poor families entering the programme was higher in better-administered regions (32.6 per cent) than in poorly administered regions (18 per cent). Apparently, wrong identification is related not so much to the inefficiency of administrative infrastructure but to the method adopted in the identification of the poor. It is significant that in states where identification was done at meetings of gram sabhas or panchayats (and not by VIPs or other bureaucrats), the degree of error was relatively low. A part of the difficulty also arose because of

the absence of any preparatory work, and the anxiety for target fulfilment.

(2) In the selection of activities, all the studies point out that no consideration was given to differences in infrastructural support, backward and forward linkages, ability of the beneficiaries, and compatibility of the scheme with the ecology of the region. Unduly large emphasis on animal husbandry programme affected the viability of the programme in some villages, apart from creating numerous other well known malpractices.

(3) Finally, credit delivery system was unsound and the attitudes of local level bank functionaries was far from satisfactory. NABARD instructions on loan maturities were flouted. Often bank officials financed only a single animal, as against two required to generate continuous income flow. Despite clear instructions, banks at local level insisted on additional security.

The impact of such a maladministered programme with so much centralisation cannot but be unsatisfactory. However, the impact cannot be regarded to be as dismal as has been made out to be in the three studies. All the three studies mechanically adopt the criterion of crossing the poverty line as a primary index of the impact of the programme, and showed how poorly the programme fared in relation to this goal. Subbarao questions the validity of such an index for assessing the impact of a programme which has barely been in existence for about 15-20 months. According to him, whether or not a particular household crossed the poverty line income level depends on (i) the initial income level of the household; (ii) investment made on the household; (iii) incremental income realised by the household; and (iv) sustained flow of income over a number of years, which in turn is a function of the level of investment and the choice of the asset, capabilities of the household, infrastructural support and demand (marketing) conditions for the final output generated.[26] The index of crossing the poverty line is inappropriate for assessing the impact of IRDP intervention, given sharp differences in the initial income level and IRDP investments of selected household across the states. This goal is rendered even more difficult owing to short run shocks inflicted by weather, technology and food prices.[27] Therefore, very poor households may be expected to climb the income ladder only gradually, even with governmental support. As such, a more reasonable index for assessing the impact of IRDP would be:[28]

(a) whether the assisted families realised higher income than the unassisted families;

(b) whether the assisted families progressively climbed to the next higher income bracket from the pre-programme income bracket; and

(c) at what cost (capital-output ratio) the above modest objectives were realised.

Unfortunately, while the test of crossing the poverty line was adopted by all the three studies, the first two indices (a) and (b) above, have not been considered.

We now turn to the question of cost effectiveness of the programme. While the NABARD study virtually ignores this aspect of the programme, there is some discussion on this aspect in the IFMR and the PEO studies. PEO study examines incremental income flow, schemewise, but unfortunately does not probe whether they differ across different situations (i.e., with better or worse infrastructure, etc.), for the same. Ratios averaged for all schemes or for all situations are difficult to interpret owing to observed inter-regional and inter-scheme variations in the income flows. The IFMR study does probe into this aspect more critically, but only for six districts over three states. Their all India average in fact is misleading.

From the IFMR study, it is possible to derive the incremental income/investment ratios, but only for one scheme, viz., the dairy (milch cow) scheme, which incidentally happens to be the most widely assisted programme. With respect to this programme, it is interesting that all the three studies stress the point that only one milch cow was financed in almost all cases even though the instructions for lending clearly provided fortwo or more milch cows. It must be stressed that both productivity and number of animals are important determinants of income flows. In many regions, animals with high productivity were just not available. If animals of poor quality are supplied, the economic efficiency of the dairy unit is bound to suffer.

The data from the three studies suggests that the capital-output ratio of 1.5, estimated by the Planning Commission, is expected to hold good only in regions where sustained amount of investment in infrastructure was already incurred. The assumed ratio of 1.5 is clearly not realistic for the backward regions. It also suggests that the returns to IRDP investments can be limited (thus lowering cost efficiency) owing to the absence of complementary scheme-related infrastructural investments. While PEO study does not relate the capital-output-ratios, the finding that emerges robustly out of this study is that the tertiary schemes were most cost-efficient in already agriculturally developed regions. As is well known, the demand for services is a positive function of per capita income. In agriculturally prosperous regions with higher per capita incomes, service activities may not face any marketing problems; their success is thus not surprising.

Sanwal points out that two important points regarding the essentials of the IRDP have been ignored in the earlier studies.[29] Firstly, the shortcoming in the choice of beneficiaries are not uniform. Rath[30] quotes from the NABARD survey that misclassification is less than one per cent in Uttar Pradesh, Bihar and Orissa; half the nation's poor are in these states. Secondly, the choice of the major activity is sound. A study undertaken by the Programme Evaluation Organisation has shown that the incremental income from dairying is about 45 per cent of the loan advanced.[31] The alternate strategy suggested by Rath, of wage employment through the NREP and the

RLEGP also suffers from distortions.[32] Those with land determine both the schemes as well as their location and benefit disproportionately from them;[33] backward areas and group are not adequately covered,[34] and the quality of the work is patchy. This is not to say that such a programme has no relevance. There is need for massive social forestry on common lands.[35]

Criticisms of IRDP need to be seen in the correct perspective so that we do not throw out the baby with the bath water.[36] The IRDP is an important policy innovation to provide productive assets to the poorest of the poor in order to generate sufficient incomes to raise them above the poverty line. The programme is central to India's development strategy of growth with redistribution. Not surprisingly, the major criticism of the programme is conceptual. The subsidy and differential rates of interest have been criticised and have been referred to as charity by those who argue that fundamental changes in the relations of production, that is land reforms, are a precondition for poverty alleviation.

Of all the programmes for rural development, the programmes for poverty alleviation are the most difficult to design and implement. Infrastructural projects like roads, rural electrification, drinking water, housing, etc. require primarily the provision of resources and technical efficiency. The projects are visible and the benefits apparent in the short term. Welfare programmes like health, education, nutrition and family welfare, etc., require primarily an efficient organisation for service delivery. These programmes also have a substantial building component. This visibility tends to cover the problems of achieving the more medium-term goals which depend on ensuring access to the service. Programmes like the IRDP and the RLEGP seek to target benefits on the poorest—the 'special publics', that is, groups in special need—as well as generate incomes. They are the most complex because they depend on the tandem effects of reliance on infrastructural service facilities provided by the State, the motivation of village-level implementers to ensure service delivery and access, as well as a positive response on the part of the 'special publics' to the assistance. The special publics cannot be reached through institutional arrangements adopted for the welfare programmes. This, in congruence, accounts for the major weakness of the anti-poverty programmes.[37]

Apart from the three studies referred to by Subbarao, Bagchee[38] refers to another study conducted by the Reserve Bank of India. According to these, it is estimated that the number of persons that have crossed the poverty line would not exceed 40 per cent of those assisted, though the individual studies give figures ranging from 17 per cent in the case of the RBI study to 49.4 per cent in the case of the PEO study. These figures, however, need to be accepted with caution due to the widely differing methodologies adopted and also as in some of the cases the incomes were discounted or the poverty line redefined in terms of current prices, while in other cases it was not done. Although the studies also point out that additional incomes had accured in the case of 55 to 90 per cent of the beneficiaries, considering that only 40 per cent of the beneficiaries (and that too on a liberal scale) had crossed the poverty line, the general conclusion that emerges is that the impact of the programme has not been satisfactory and that there is a need to make the IRDP more effective.[39]

These studies also identify the following two specific findings of the programme: (i) there was wrong identification of the beneficiaries to the extent of 15 to 20 per cent at an all India level, though this ranged from 47 per cent to 70 per cent in different states. This has been treated as one of the major shortcomings of the IRDP.[40] (ii) The selection of activities was wrongly done without any consideration being given to the ability of the beneficiaries, differences in infrastructural support, backward and forward linkages, etc. As a result of all these, the activities did not prove to be viable, thereby affecting the impact of the programme.

In addition, these studies make certain observations regarding the planning process and the organisation available for implementing the programme. In the former category are the adoption of a uniform strategy throughout the country, disregarding differences in the level of infrastructural development and incidence of poverty, inflexibility of the programme, standardisation of operations, uniform procedures for all allocations, etc. In the latter are the organisational and administrative weaknesses, both in terms of lack of qualified and trained staff at various levels and organisations, as well as mechanisms to coordinate and integrate between these organisations so as to make the implementation effective.

While most of the studies quoted above have listed out the specific shortcomings and categorised them as either administrative failures or weaknesses in planning procedures, in fact, these shortcomings are basically the result of not properly analysing the environment, including the available organisation, in order to formulate an operational strategy and generate a realistic design of the programmes. Furthermore, as beneficiaries are a part of the environment, this would also require that the beneficiaries, even though they might have been defined in terms of general characteristics, be studied in detail to segment them into more homogeneous groups. Such an analysis would help in dealing with the crucial issue whether all segments should be served at the same time and whether they require to be provided with the same service. Moreover, it also helps to understand the problems in regard to supply of services to the different segments considering the degree of diversity of the environment, the problem of logistics and the adequacy of institutions with which the programme is to operate. It is only after considering these issues that a viable strategy can be formulated.[41] Samuel rightly remarks,[42] "when an environment's complexity increases, the strategic choices must reflect this. Similarly, the more complex the objectives of a programme, the greater the attention to be paid to its strategy. When conflicting multiple objectives are to be achieved, strategic choices become increasingly difficult. Under these conditions, programme leaders tend to reduce complexity by limiting their goals. They can phase the accomplishment of multiple goals by first focusing on a dominant goal. The stimultaneous pursuit of diverse goals requires management of diverse services or outputs leading to severe organisation overload. The conflicts and the mounting demands on the time and skills of top management then spells disaster for the programme. Only through a careful analysis of the complexity of objectives given by the government and the complexity of the environment can the operating goals of the programme be determined. This is the first and basic strategic choice that faces a development programme."

In the context of the above quotation, the failure of the poverty alleviation programme appears to be as a consequence of not taking into account the complexities of the environment of having multiple and conflicting objectives instead of simplifying them by focusing on a single operational goal and designing a suitable and viable strategy on this basis. The pursuit of multiple goals without taking into account the organisational capabilities and attempting to provide diverse services has spelled disaster for the programmes. One look at the extent of activities involved in the IRDP would make this amply clear. These include identification of beneficiaries, selection of viable economic activities, procurement of suitable assets, obtaining of loans from banks, inculcating stills in the beneficiaries to operate these assets by training them, ensuring infrastructural support for the activity, marketing of the produce, etc., a whole range of varied activities, and what is more important, their integration— a very difficult process which is referred to as "backward and forward linkages" and is, if the guidelines are to be believed, to be achieved through exhortations. The original concept of the IRDP was, however, different as it visualised the IRDP as a total development plan for the block based on local resources and their productive use rather than as an individual beneficiary-oriented programme. Whether such a programme would have been successful or not cannot be stated with any certainty but it must be remembered that it was proposed to be introduced in only 2,000 blocks as a pilot scheme and that too with the necessary block-level planning paraphernalia. However, pending the setting up of this machinery, as an interim step, it was decided to begin with the identification of the rural poor and preparing plans for their development. But while block-level planning did not materialise, this interim programme was continued and extended without adequate thought as to whether it was possible to properly implement a programme of this magnitude and ramification with the existing framework.[43]

As pointed out earlier, Dantwala[44] and Hirway[45] both feel that Rath lays too much emphasis on the role of wage employment in the strategy of poverty alleviation. While the former is of the view that this will lead to the total dependence of the poor on the employers, the latter states that such an approach ignores the fact that self-employment is a major form of employment in the rural economy. Moreover, they both feel that Rath in his advocacy of wage employment tends to ignore the malpractices that occur in rural employment programmes and also the fact that they accentuate the gap between the rich and the poor by strengthening the asset base of those who are relatively better off.

There is however, no basic difference in all these approaches and the difference, if any, is due to the greater emphasis on either self-employment or wage employment, as all of them agree that both these kinds of programmes should form components of the poverty alleviation strategy. The actual mix between the transfer of assets and skills approach and the employment approach will depend on the circumstanees prevailing and would have to be taken into account while preparing the micro-level plan. However, it should be pointed out that at present there is no integration between these two elements, though they form two facets of poverty alleviation, as the IRDP and the rural employment programmes are planned and implemented in isolation of one another, even though the field agency as well as the administrative machinery are the same. This integration should have, in fact, emerged from the design of both the programmes rather than leaving it to the field level agency to attempt it, depending on the perceptions of the implementers. As a result of this, it cannot be said that there is any conscious strategy in existence in respect of these two components.[46]

An overall reading of the Seventh Plan document leads to the surmise that the basic emphasis is on the generation of productive employment rather than the alleviation of poverty, which was the primary objective of the Sixth Plan. The programme for poverty alleviation should be regarded as supplementing the basic plan for overall economic growth in terms of generating productive assets and skills as well as incomes for the poor.[47] In its approach to the problem of poverty, though the plan document does take cognisance of the debate referred to above on whether wage-employment programmes should be given priority over self-employment schemes, it does not come to any conclusion. In fact, the discussion skirts the main issues and ignores the critical findings of the evaluation studies. For instance, it argues that in general, the IRDP performance has been better in not only relatively more developed regions but also in other areas where followup measures had been undertaken and the people involved through their representatives. Moreover, it is of the view that household enterprises are economically viable as they exist on a wide scale through all the regions and constitute a major source of employment. According to the Plan, the only constraints that such units suffer from is in the supply of raw materials, credit and marketing. It therefore states that once this is assured and as long as the overall economic growth is satisfactory, there will be adequate demand for products manufactured or produced by these rural households and thus there is no cause for pessimism. Such an analysis, however, does not appear to be correct as it assumes that all the rural households are equally endowed with assets, capabilities, skills and entrepreneurial abilities and ignores the findings of the various field studies.[48]

In short, the Plan's reading on the situation is that the failure of these programmes is basically due to the administrative weaknesses and is not due to any shortcomings in the programme design. It is, therefore, of the view that the change in strategy required is in the organisational domain and that by merely affecting these changes it would be possible to provide the necessary forward and backward linkages and assist all the poor househols to cross the poverty line. Towards this end, it plans a three-pronged strategy of, firstly, decentralising programme formulation and implementation through local bodies so as to ensure proper selection of projects and beneficiaries; secondly, strengthening the administrative machinery and suitably training it, and thirdly, taking up group-oriented activities through cooperatives, informal groups, etc.

However, this analysis does not appear to be valid firstly, because the premise that all household enterprises are economically viable is a questionable one, and secondly, it is not merely by making some peripheral changes in the organisation, but by dealing with the basic conceptual issues and problems underlying the programmes that they can be made more effective.

Criticising on the fundamental aspect of the IRDP, Guhan[49] is of the view that a publicly funded and manageable, administratively viable and financially feasible social security system must be an essential component of an anti-poverty package to take care of the poorest. According to him, the low-end poverty in its worst forms cannot be ameliorated by providing them with opportunities for self-employment or wage employment. The worst placed among the poor are those who are not able to participate in economic activity on account of old age, physical and mental handicaps, various disabilities due to morbidity, etc. These contingencies need to be relieved by measures that are specifically directed towards the target groups. In the absence or inadequacy of such measures, the burden has to be borne, if at all, by the families, relatives and local communities of those affected. Informal social security of this kind shifts the hardship to those who are themselves most often under the poverty line and ill-placed to support dependents. Increasingly, community and familial support cultures and systems are also weakening.

Kurien's line of thinking on IRDP shows a positive indication. According to him there is nothing singularly bad about the IRDP. Also it is not a panancea for all our ills. The truth is in between the extremes.[50]

Notes and References

1. Saxena, A.P., "Concurrent evaluation of IRDP: selected aspects for administrative followup", Economic and Political Weekly, Vol. XXII, No. 39, Sept. 26, 1987, Review of Agriculture, p. A-121.

2. For details see the Sixth Five Year Plan document, Planning Commission, Government of India, 1980-85.

3. The poverty line income is defined as an income not exceeding Rs. 3500 per annum per family comprising, on an average, of five individuals. The poverty line income has lately been revised to Rs. 6400 per annum per family according to a circular issued by the Ministry of Agriculture, Department of Rural Development, Government of India. The cut off point has been fixed at Rs. 4800 per annum per family.

4. This methodology, adopted by the Government of India, is based on the socio-economic conditions criterion of different categories, apart from their demographic characteristics.

5. See the Annual Report of the Department of Rural Development, Ministry of Agriculture, Government of India, 1985-86 and the Seventh Five Year Plan document, Planning Commission, Government of India, 1985-90.

6. Rath, Nilakantha, " 'Garibi Hatao', Can IRDP do it?", Economic and Political Weekly, Vol. XX, No. 6, Feb. 9, 1985, p. 238.

7. Refer to the discussion on Rath's paper by Indira Hirway in Economic and Political Weekly, Vol. XX, No. 13, March 30, 1985, p. 561.

8. Ahuja, Kanta and Pradeep Bhargava, "Integrated rural development programme, an evaluation: Jaipur district", mimeograph, Jaipur Institute of Development Studies, 1984.

   Also see the Report of Canara Bank, "Impact study on IRDP in Tirunelveli and Periyar district (TN)", Bangalore, 1984; Jain, S.C., "Impact study of integrated rural development programme, Uchchhal Taluk, Surat (Gujarat)", mimeograph, South Gujarat University, 1983; Jain, S.C., "Impact study on integrated rural development, Bardoli Taluk (Gujarat)", mimeograph, South Gujarat University, 1983; Report of National Bank of Agricultural and Rural Development (NABARD); "Study of the implementation of integrated rural development programme", mimeograph, Bombay, 1984; Report of State Bank of Bikaner and Jaipur,

"Evaluation study of the IRDP beneficiaries in Bikaner and Jaipur (Rajasthan)", mimeograph, Jaipur; Report of the State Bank of Hyderabad, "Monitoring-cum-mid term evaluation of IRDP", mimeograph, Hyderabad, 1983; Report of the Evaluation Division of the State Planning Board, Kerala, "Integrated rural development programme: an evaluation study", mimeograph, October, 1981.

9. Refer to the NABARD study on the "implementation of integrated rural development programme", mimeograph, Bombay, 1984.
10. Op. cit. (6), p. 245.
11. Op. cit. (7), p. 562.
12. Refer to the Draft Report of the 32nd round of NSS (July 1977-June 1978). It shows that the percentage of self-employed in the working force (either in principal or subsidiary capacity) according to usual status in rural India was 62.52, National Sample Survey, New Delhi, 1982.
13. Hirway argues that it will be difficult to define both the categories in a clear-cut fashion, though broadly it can be said that assetless unskilled labour will prefer wage-employment. NSS data on employment and unemployment and related matters can provide this information. However, it will be necessary to redesign the sampling in such a way that the data are made available at the district level also.
14. Op. cit. (6), p. 241.
15. Op. cit. (7), p. 562.
16. Hirway, Indira, "Programmes for poverty eradication: a critique of target group approach", Sardar Patel Institute of Economic and Social Research. mimeograph, Ahmedabad, 1983. The study examines the process of percolation of target group programmes and observes that because of the economic, social and power-based stratification of the rural society, the poorest three deciles had received little from the programmes.
17. Various evaluation studies of public works programmes have shown this. For example, refer to D.P. Apte, "CSRE for rural employment: evaluation of the programme in a district in Maharashtra", Economic and Political Weekly, March 4, 1973; G.B. Rogers, "Effects of public works on rural poverty: some case studies for the Kosi area of Bihar", Economic and Political Weekly, February, 1973. Also see the Report of the Programmes Evaluation Organisation, "A study of special employment programmes", Planning Commission, Government of India, New Delhi, 1979.

18. Hirway, Indira, "Special employment programmes in rural development: a study of NREP in Gujarat", Sardar Patel Institute of Economic and Social Research, mimeograph, Ahmedabad, 1984. The study shows that data on poverty and unemployment were not taken into consideration while allocating NREP funds to talukas and villages. Political leaders were observed to be playing an important role in decision-making.
19. Subbarao, K., "Regional variations in impact of anti-poverty programmes: a review of evidence", Economic and Political Weekly, Vol XX, No. 43, October 26, 1985, p. 1829.
20. National Bank for Agriculture and Rural Development (NABARD), "Study of implementation of IRDP", mimeograph, 1984.
21. Programmes Evaluation Organisation (PEO), "Evaluation report on integrated rural development programme", Planning Commission, Government of India, New Delhi, 1985.
22. Institute for Financial Management and Research (IFMR), "An economic assessment of poverty eradication and rural unemployment alleviation programme and their prospects", mimeograph, Madras, 1984.
23. Op. cit. (19), p. 1829.
24. For details of methodology, refer the preface of the PEO study.
25. Op. cit. (19), p. 1830.
26. Ibid.
27. It is useful to recall that the data of NCAER All India Rural Income Survey of 1968-69, 1969-70 and 1970-71 showed that the year to year fluctuations in real income profiles of poor households were highly sensitive to food price changes and weather. See also I. Adelman, K. Subbarao and P.S. Vashishtha, "Some dynamic aspects of rural poverty in India", Economic and Political Weekly, Review of Agriculture, September 28, 1985.
28. Op. cit. (19), p. 1830.
29. Sanwal, Mukul, "Garibi Hatao: improving implementation", Economic and Political Weekly, Vol. XX, No. 49, Dec. 7, 1985, p. 2176.
30. Op. cit. (6).
31. Programme Evaluation Organisation, "Evaluation study of small farmers, marginal farmers and agricultural labourers project", Planning Commission, Government of India, New Delhi, 1974-75.
32. Dantwala, M.L., "Garibi hatao: strategy options", Economic and Political Weekly, Vol. XX, No. 11, March 16, 1985.
33. Programme Evaluation Organisation, "Joint evaluation report on employment guarantee scheme of Maharashtra (April 1976-October

1978)", Planning Commission, Government of India, New Delhi, and Directorate of Economics and Statistics, Government of Maharashtra, Bombay, 1980.

34. Hirway, Indira, Background paper on a Seminar on Special Employment Programmes in Rural Development, Gandhi Labour Institute, Ahmedabad, January 12, 1985.

35. Sanwal, Mukul, "Design of hill development: lessons from the Plains of Uttar Pradesh and Himachal Pradesh", Economic and Political Weekly, Vol. XVIII, No. 7, February 12, 1985.

36. Op. cit. (29), p. 2176.

37. Ibid.

38. Bagchee Sandeep, "Poverty alleviation programmes in the Seventh Plan: an appraisal", Economic and Political Weekly, Vol. XXII, No. 4, January 24, 1987.

39. This view has been expressed by Subbarao, who criticises the basic methodology of the IRDP which takes into account the poverty line criterion for evaluating the performance of the programme. Bagchee, however, sticks to this criterion on the pretext that this was an objective set by the programme itself. If the ultimate achievement, according to him, was subject to a number of assumptions, the objective should have been stated differently.

40. Bagchee also uses the data of the first round survey of concurrent evaluation of IRDP undertaken by different organisations in the country, on behalf of the Department of Rural Development, Ministry of Agriculture, Government of India, New Delhi, Oct. 1986.

41. Op. cit. (38), p. 140.

42. Paul, Samuel, "Strategic management of development programmes: guidelines for action", International Labour Office, Geneva, 1983.

43. Op. cit. (38), p. 140.

44. Op. cit. (32).

45. Op. cit. (7).

46. Op. cit. (38).

47. The Seventh Five Year Plan document (1985-90), Planning Commission, Government of India, New Delhi, October 1985, Vol. 1, p. 50,

48. Subbarao in his analysis has indicated that the success of the IRDP is related to the initial income levels of the assisted households and therefore, to their asset endowment as well as to the level of infrastructure development in the region.

49. Guhan, S., "Reaching out to the poor", Economic Times, Silver Jubilee Special, Dec. 19, 1986. Also see Guhan's article, "Rural poverty: policy and play acting", Economic and Political Weekly, November 22, 1988.

50. Kurien, N.J., "IRDP: how relevant is it?", Economic and Political Weekly, Vol. XXII, No. 52, Dec. 26, 1987.

5

Concurrent Evaluation of IRDP

The Integrated Rural Development Programme was introduced in a modest way during the Fifth Five Year Plan. During the Sixth Plan, it was extended to cover the entire rural areas of the country and during the Seventh Plan, it continues to be the centre piece of the anti-poverty programmes.[1] The fundamental objective of the IRDP is to enable the rural poor cross the poverty line through the provision of assets which are income generating.[2] More than 16.5 million families were assisted during the Sixth Plan. In the Seventh Plan, the target of assistance as well as the fund allocation is much higher.[3]

A review of studies on IRDP given in the preceding chapter shows that IRDP has been a much talked about programme. It has caught the attention of numerous researchers and academicians which is evident from the number of materials, both in the form of articles and reports, written on it. The vast majority of the researches have been rather critical of the programme, although they fail to take heed to the fact that the programme has not had a long existence, and any evaluation, whatsoever, should consider this erucial aspect of the programme's longevity. Subbarao, in his review, has, however, made a passing reference to this.[4] There are vehement critics whose arguments appear quite logical, and referring to them in this chapter, would be a mere repetition of what has already been discussed. Some of the criticisms point to the methodological weaknesses of the programme, while others refer justifiably to the implementation loopholes and administrative pitfalls.

Methodology

The analyses and discussions of the various issues involved here (in this chapter) are based on the massive primary data/information generated by the Concurrent Evaluation Survey of IRDP.[5] This novel scheme of data collection by non-government agencies for monitoring the implementation of the programme and evaluating its impact on the beneficiaries was the result of wide criticism of the implementation of the programme during the Sixth Plan. Though most of the shortcomings of the IRDP were known to the concerned implementing agencies and the public at large as a result of experience and on the basis of various localised and micro-level evaluation studies, a national level debate of a serious nature[6] took place only after the publication of a few evaluation studies of all India coverage.[7]

The concurrent evaluation survey was carried out during the period January to December 1987. All the districts in the country were covered in this survey. In each district, a sample of 40 IRDP beneficiaries were studied in detail. The method of sampling followed was a stratified four-stage random scheme. A combination of interview, observation and verification of records was used for filling up the pre-coded and structured household schedule, specifically prepared for this pupose by an expert group. Apart from collecting objective data, an attempt was made to look at the programme from the point of view of the beneficiaries. Hence a few pointed questions were included in the schedule to ascertain the perception of the beneficiaries about some of the critical points. Though the survey covered both current as well as old beneficiaries, some of the data/information were specific only to the beneficiaries who were assisted two years before the survey. The total sample size of such beneficiaries was 16,616, spreated over all the states and union territories of the country.

The IRDP Assistance

According to the IRDP circular, the selection of the beneficiary was based on the Antyodya principle, whereby the selection was supposed to begin from the poorest of the poor families. Thus, the IRDP beneficiaries have been divided into (a) the destitutes, with annual family income ranging between Re. 1 and Rs. 2,265; (b) the very very poor, with income ranging between Rs. 2,266 and Rs. 3,500; (c) the very poor, with income ranging between Rs. 3,501 and Rs. 4,800 and (d) the poor, with income ranging between Rs. 4,801 and Rs. 6,400. Another group, in the income category of Rs. 6,400 and above has also been taken for the purpose of the survey, to make accommodation for the non-poor, who have also been included in the list of beneficiaries in some of the states.

The poverty line income of Rs. 3,500 per annum for an average family of five members continued to be the official cut-off level for IRDP assistance throughout the Sixth Plan period, even though the purchasing power of rupee was significantly eroded by inflation since 1977-78.[8] It was only during the Seventh Plan that the poverty line income was revised to Rs. 6,400 per annum per family.[9] The true pre-assistance incomes of the sample beneficiaries as assessed by the investigators of the research institution which conducted the survey are presented in table 5.1.

It is evident from the table that at the national level, only 71 per cent of the sample beneficiaries had pre-assistance income below Rs. 3,500, which means that 71 per cent of the sample benficiaries were below the poverty line and the rest 29 per cent were above it, although their names too had been included in the list of beneficiaries. At the national level, out of the 71 per cent beneficiaries who satisfied the eligibility criterion according to official guidelines, 25 per cent belonged

Table 5.1

Distribution of Income at the Time of Assistance

(Percentage of total at each level)

	Rupees							
	1-2,265	*2,266-3,500*	*1-3,500*	*3,501-4,800*	*1-4,800*	*4,801-6,400*	*>6,400*	*Total*
1	*2*	*3*	*4*	*5*	*6*	*7*	*8*	*9*
Andhra Pradesh	13	48	61	29	90	6	4	100
Assam	5	21	26	36	62	18	20	100
Bihar	33	40	73	20	93	2	5	100
Gujarat	3	72	75	21	96	4	0	100
Haryana	15	55	70	25	95	4	1	100
Himachal Pradesh	50	36	86	7	93	4	3	100
Jammu and Kashmir	26	70	96	3	99	1	0	100
Karnataka	42	44	86	10	96	0	4	100
Kerala	42	48	90	10	100	0	0	100

(*Contd.*)

1	*2*	*3*	*4*	*5*	*6*	*7*	*8*	*9*
Madhya Pradesh	27	55	82	14	96	3	1	100
Maharashtra	28	53	81	13	94	4	2	100
Manipur	3	35	38	37	75	17	8	100
Meghalaya	46	43	89	11	100	0	0	100
Nagaland	15	40	55	26	82	8	10	100
Orissa	45	39	84	12	96	2	2	100
Punjab	6	24	30	60	90	2	2	100
Rajasthan	34	38	72	19	91	8	3	100
Sikkim	80	20	100	0	100	6	0	100
Tamil Nadu	32	50	82	14	96	0	1	100
Tripura	0	23	23	63	86	3	3	100
Uttar Pradesh	10	44	54	35	89	11	4	100
West Bengal	8	38	46	44	90	7	2	100
Union Territories	13	32	45	32	77	8	8	100
National average	25	46	71	21	92	15	3	100

to the income group Re. 1-2,265 who are categorised as 'destitutes' and the remaining 46 per cent belonged to the income group Rs. 2,265-3,500, who are categorised as 'very very poor'. Of the 29 per cent non-eligible beneficiaries, 21 per cent belonged to the income group Rs. 3,501-4,800, who are categorised as 'very poor' and are treated as eligible for assistance during the Seventh Plan. Out of the remaining 8 per cent non-eligible beneficiaries, 5 per cent belonged to the income group Rs. 4,800-6,400 and the balance 3 per cent had pre-assistance income more than Rs. 6,400, which is the revised poverty line for the Seventh Plan. It may be observed in this connection that the four national level evaluation studies of IRDP[10] had reported assistance of non-eligible beneficiaries ranging from 15 to 26 per cent as against 29 per cent in the present survey.

The level of conformity to official guidelines varied significantly across the states. In some states like Chandigarh and Tripura, more than 50 per cent of the beneficiaries were ineligible for assistance, that is, belonged to the income group Rs. 3,501 and above. On the contrary, in certain states like Sikkim, 80 per cent beneficiaries belonged to the income group Re. 1-3,500. Even if a more liberal eligibility criterion[11] is used, the eligible beneficiaries will still be much below the 100 per cent mark. The coverage of families from the income group Rs. 3,501-4,800 was between 60-62 per cent in Tripura, Chandigarh and Punjab, 43 per cent in West Bengal, 34-36 per cent in Manipur, Assam, Mizoram and Uttar Pradesh, 27-28 per cent in Andhra Pradesh, Nagaland and Lakshadweep and 25 per cent in Dadra and Nagar Haveli. Thus, the total coverage of families from the income group Re. 1-4,800 was 92 per cent. The rest 8 per cent were from the income group Rs. 4,800 and above. At the national level, 5 per cent families whose income was between Rs. 4,801-6,400 and 3 per cent families whose income was more than Rs. 6,400 had been assisted due to an under-recording of their incomes. Such families were not eligible for receiving assistance even from the point of view of the new cut-off criterion of the Seventh Plan. About 32 per cent families in Andaman and Nicobar Islands, 15-20 per cent in Chandigarh, Assam, Manipur and Mizoram, 10-12 per cent in Delhi, Tripura and Pondicherry and less than 10 per cent in other states had been assisted from the income group Rs. 4,801-6,400. Similarly, 75 per cent families in Delhi, 10-17 per cent in Assam, Mizoram, Nagaland and Chandigarh and 5-7 per cent in Bihar, Andhra Pradesh and Manipur had been assisted from the income group Rs. 6,400 and above. The example of Delhi where 75 per cent of beneficiaries were ineligible for assistance, is a case in point. Two reasons could be adduced to this state of affairs: one, that in the context of the Sixth Plan target of assisting 3,000 beneficiaries per block, it might have been difficult, especially by the final year of the Plan to identify enough number of families belonging to the 'destitute' and 'very very poor' groups in the more prosperous blocks;[12] second, there was some kind of methodological flaw in the process of selection of the eligible families.

Table 5.2 gives the incomewise breakup of the women, scheduled caste and the scheduled tribe beneficiaries at the national level.

Table 5.2

Incomewise Breakup among Women, SC and ST Beneficiaries

National level percentage of beneficiaries in different annual income groups					
	Re. 1-2265	*Rs. 2,266-3,500*	*Rs. 3,501-4,800*	*Rs. 4,801-6,400*	*>Rs. 6,400*
Women	32	45	17	5	1
Scheduled Caste	25	45	16	4	2
Scheduled Tribe	28	47	17	5	3

It is clear from the table that about 75 per cent of the beneficiaries from among the three categories, namely, women, scheduled caste and scheduled tribe were getting genuine assistance, if one were to take the Sixth Plan poverty line income criterion. In the income group Re. 1-4,800, this percentage further increased to 94 each for women and scheduled caste beneficiaries and 92 for the scheduled tribe beneficiaries. This points to the fact that these categories are not being ignored compared to beneficiaries belonging to the general category, and that they are being treated at par with the beneficiaries of the general category, so far as IRDP assistance is concerned.

Process of Selection

As per the official guidelines, the list of identified potential beneficiaries prepared by the officials has to be presented in the gram sabha meeting and got ratified by it before they are actually assisted.[18] This is to ensure that the most deserving poor get priority over others and that no non-poor or non-eligible families get IRDP assistance through suppression of incomes or through collusion with government functioneries. However, in actual practice, this procedure of public participation and open selection does not take place everywhere.

The distribution of sample beneficiaries according to the mode of selection is given in table 5.3. The table reveals that at the national level, 59 per cent of the beneficiaries were selected in the gram sabha meetings, 38 per cent by officials and the remaining 3 per cent by others including MPs and MLAs. The statewise breakup of selection of beneficiaries shows that in Himachal Pradesh, Sikkim, Tripura and West Bengal, all the beneficiaries were selected in the gram sabha meeting. In case of Gujarat, Haryana, Kerala, Meghalaya, Orissa and Rajasthan, such selection was to the extent of 90-99 per cent. On the contrary, in states like Assam, Bihar and Tamil Nadu, between 78-88 per cent of the selection was made by the officials. In Maharashtra, 50 per cent of the beneficiaries were selected by the officials, which was higher than the percentage of selection made in the gram sabha meeting (39 per cent). The percentage of selection made by others including MPs and MLAs was as high as 15 in Jammu and Kashmir followed by 12 per cent in Tamil Nadu and 11 per cent in

Maharashtra. Incidentally, Tamil Nadu has the lowest percentage of beneficiaries selected in the gram sabha meeting.

Table 5.3

Statewise Breakup of Selection of Potential Beneficiaries

State	*Percentage of beneficiaries selected*			
	Gram Sabha	*Officials*	*Others*	*Total*
Andhra Pradesh	58	37	5	100
Assam	15	85	0	100
Bihar	8	88	4	100
Gujarat	99	1	0	100
Haryana	90	9	1	100
Himachal Pradesh	100	0	0	100
Jammu and Kashmir	48	37	15	100
Karnataka	78	19	2	100
Kerala	99	1	0	100
Madhya Pradesh	41	57	2	100
Maharashtra	39	50	11	100
Manipur	58	39	3	100
Meghalaya	99	1	0	100
Nagaland	51	44	5	100
Orissa	98	2	0	100
Punjab	85	7	8	100
Rajasthan	97	1	2	100
Sikkim	100	0	0	100
Tamil Nadu	10	78	12	100
Tripura	100	0	0	100
Uttar Pradesh	85	15	0	100
West Bengal	100	0	0	100
Union Territories	57	35	8	100
National Average	59	38	3	100

If we compare tables 5.1 and 5.3, there seems to be a close association between gram sabha selection and the proportion of genuine beneficiaries. In Sikkim, 100 per cent of the selection took place in the gram sabha meetings and 80 per cent of the beneficiaries were selected from the category of the 'destitutes'. In states like Gujarat, Haryana, Himachal Pradesh, Kerala, Meghalaya and Orissa, where a high percentage beneficiaries were selected in the gram sabha meeting, more beneficiaries were selected from the category of the 'destitutes' as well as the 'very very poor'. This supports the contention that in the meeting of the gram sabha, objectivity in the selection of beneficiaries is largely followed, which also underscores the need for more public participation in the selection for IRDP assistance.[14]

Delays in Providing Assistance

The process involved in the application for loan, sanctioning of loan and the actual receipt of the asset is not only cumbersome from the point of view of the beneficiary, but is equally time-consuming. The beneficiary not only has to meet his daily requirements, but also has to move from his place of residence to the block office, from the block office to the bank, from the bank to other office/markets, etc. This wastes a lot of his time, which he could have otherwise utilised in other useful work. The total time wasted from the day the application is made by the beneficiary to the day the asset is received by him, on an average, is worked out at 129 days, which includes the block delay, the bank delay as well as the delay in the grounding of the asset. The delay at each stage has been shown in table 5.4. The block delay refers to the timelag between the date of receipt of the application in the block and the date of forwarding it to the bank. The national average of the block delay was 29 days. The table shows that the block delay was more than three months in Assam and Nagaland. This could be explained by the fact that the block level machinery in these two states is not very well developed, owing, probably, to the lack of infrastructural development, vis-a-vis, the other states. In case of Delhi too, the delay at

Table 5.4

Delays in Allotment

States	*Average delays at different states*
	Block delay (no. of days)
Nagaland	97
Assam	92
Delhi	75
Punjab	53
Chandigarh	46
National average	29
	Bank delay (no. of days)
Andhra Pradesh and Jammu & Kashmir	145
West Bengal	118
Assam	102
Andaman and Nicobar Islands	90
Orissa	79
National average	66
	Grounding delay
Andaman and Nicobar Islands	104
Assam	79
West Bengal	66
Kerala and Rajasthan	63
Madhya Pradesh	59
National average	34

the block level was as much as 75 days, which probably has been due to the negligence of the block level authorities, deliberate or undeliberate. The bank delay refers to the time-lag between the date of forwarding the loan application by the block to the bank and the date of sanction of loan by the bank. The national average of the bank delay was 66 days.

Four states, namely Andhra Pradesh, Jammu and Kashmir, West Bengal and Assam took three months or more in sanctioning the loan. No justification can be given to such callous attitude of the bankers in these states. Granted that banks are hard pressed for time owing to a number of activities they have to perform simultaneously. They are even understaffed. But then, it is basically a question of priorities, and if banks involved in IRDP financing had realised the importance of a programme like the IRDP, such a delay would not have come about. The delay in grounding the asset has been taken as the time lag between the date of sanction of loan and the date of actual receipt of the asset by the beneficiary. The national average of this delay was about 34 days. In states like Assam, West Bengal, Kerala and Rajasthan and in Andaman and Nicobar Islands, this delay was of more than three months. Some justification in this delay is understood. For example, if a beneficiary has applied for a milch cow, the cow will be handed over to him after the necessary formalities of its purchase are made and its quality (in terms of its health and milk-generating capacity, etc.) is assessed. This would normally take time, depending upon the availability of the animal in the market, procurement of health certificate from the veterinary office, etc. Nevertheless, a delay of more than a month is unpardonable, and needs to be seriously looked into.

The delays in IRDP assistance can be counter-productive to the basic objectives of the programme. On the face of it, the delays appear to be largely administrative and procedural. Block level delays could be due to time consuming procedures, number of clearances required, cross referencing, financial vetting or sheer inefficiency.[15] Bank delays could be due to lengthy procedures and formalities before sanctions. One even suspects that part of the bank delays could well be due to a continuing commercial posture as against the needed developmental approach. A beneficiary below the poverty line can hardly be expected to comply with the paper work, much less provide any guarantees, references or any proof of capacity to repay. Perhaps the points stipulated on the decision line are so many that the beneficiary can well be reduced to a full time runner from office to office rather than following his own vocation.

The seriousness of the delays and its implication is reinforced by the number of visits the beneficiary has to necessarily make to sort out pending matters with the block and the bank. The concurrent evaluation provides details about the number of days, and the amount spent by the beneficiary in visiting various offices and markets in connection with the assistance. The average number of days spent by the beneficiary in going to the bank, block, other offices and markets in connection with the assistance has been indicated in Table 5.5. The table shows that at the national level, four days were spent by the beneficiaries in going to the bank, two days at the block, one day in visiting various offices and two days in the markets. In Jammu and Kashmir, 25 days were spent in going to the bank, 16 days at the block, 12 days in visiting various offices and 10 days in the markets. Even in Delhi and Haryana, these figures were much higher than the national average. The beneficiaries have therefore to incur some out of pocket expenditure on the trips to the block office, bank, other offices and market in connection with the assistance. The amount spent on such visits has been shown in Table 5.6. The table shows that at the national level, 66 per cent of the beneficiaries spent upto Rs. 50 on such visits. All the beneficiaries in Sikkim and Tripura spent upto Rs. 50 on such visits. The percentage was also very high in Arunachal Pradesh, Meghalaya, Orissa, West Bengal, Goa and Mizoram. The percentage of beneficiaries spending between Rs. 51-100 was 23 at the national level. In Uttar Pradesh, 41 per cent of the beneficiaries spent between Rs. 51-100 on such visits. Again, at the national level, 11 per cent of the beneficiaries spent more than Rs. 100. In Delhi, the percentage of such beneficiaries was as high as 55 followed by Jammu and Kashmir (46 per cent) and Lakshadweep (41 per cent).

The problem of lead time is thus serious and clearly has an unproductive impact on the beneficiaries as well as on the programme as a whole. It therefore needs to be investigated

Table 5.5

Average Number of Days Spent on Visits

State	*Average no. of days spent by the beneficiary*
	Bank
Jammu and Kashmir	25
Delhi	9
Haryana	8
Assam	6
Andhra Pradesh	5
National average	4
	Block
Jammu and Kashmir	16
Delhi	13
Arunachal Pradesh	4
Assam and Tripura	3
Kerala	2
National average	2
	Other Offices
Jammu and Kashmir	12
Delhi	3
Haryana	2
Maharashtra and Rajasthan	1
National average	1
	Markets
Jammu and Kashmir and Haryana	10
Tripura, Uttar Pradesh, Andaman and Nicobar Islands and Delhi	2
National average	2

Table 5.6
Amount Spent on Visits

State	*Amount spent on visits to different places*
	Percentage of beneficiaries spending less than Rs. 50
Sikkim and Tripura	100
Arunachal Pradesh and Meghalaya	94-95
Orissa, West Bengal, Goa and Mizoram	90-91
Punjab, Chandigarh and Manipur	87-88
Himachal Pradesh	82
National level	86
	Percentage of beneficiaries spending between Rs. 51-100
Uttar Pradesh	41
Haryana and Tamil Nadu	36-37
Maharashtra	30
Karnataka	26
Assam and Bihar	23
National level	23
	Percentage of beneficiaries spending more than Rs. 100
Delhi	55
Jammu and Kashmir	46
Lakshadweep	41
Haryana	29
Tamil Nadu	24
National level	11

in detail. Initially comprehensive work flow analysis should be conducted in typically bad cases to isolate the reasons for the delays which could be (a) administrative, highlighted by prescribed procedures, inadequate staff support at the block level, referencing for securing approvals or (b) attitudinal, due to inadequate concern for the beneficiary and inability to see the programme in terms of its developmental objectives. It could be a feature of an increasingly pervasive bureaucratic apathy and cynicism—a fall out of a culture which intrinisically continues to relish a regulatory style and is neither responsive to the ethos of development nor is concerned with the inherent compulsions of change.[16] Sufficient field analysis will therefore be required to pinpoint the key blocks at the local level leading to sound remedial measures.

Over-valuation of Assets

The criticisms at the stage of the implementation of the IRDP revolve around corruption, malpractices, bribery and other leakages. Extreme forms of corruption and malpractices are the cases where the government functionaries and bankers involved in the implementation of the programme, in connivance with the beneficiary, dispose off the asset immediately after the asset is purchased and share the subsidy component of the assistance. Such cases are very rare, and the beneficiaries who are involved are, by and large, not aware of the long run implications of such a connivance. A lesser but more common type of corruption is the payment of bribes by the beneficiary from his own resources to the individual functionaries of the government or bank, who are involved in processing the application and acquiring the asset. The former type of corruption is very rare, especially in well-administered states.[17] The latter is quite common in a number of states, believably, but the information is extremely difficult to elicit and the amounts involved are difficult to quantify.[18]

According to the guidelines, the asset has to be purchased by a committee consisting of the representatives of the block, bank and the beneficiary. In a vast majority of cases the assets were purchased by a purchase committee.[19] In actual practice, however, the involvement of the beneficiary in the purchase decision, especially about the price is rather minimal. Often at times the price would be highly inflated, or the quality of the asset would be highly substandard, if the price was fixed. The difference would be shared by the various parties involved, on the basis of a predetermined formula.[20] Another reason for higher prices for IRDP assets is the market process itself. When a scheme becomes popular in a particular area, the market value of the asset under this scheme goes up, and the greater the demand for this asset under the IRDP scheme, the greater becomes its price.[21] It is, in fact, the IRDP component attached to an asset that makes its values higher in the market, in comparison to the price the same asset would fetch in the market under normal conditions.

To capture the extent of excess cost the beneficiary is likely to incur, due to the possibility of a higher price he has to pay for an asset, the beneficiary was asked to give his estimate of the value of the asset when it was acquired. The difference between the cost as per the purchase record and the value of the asset as perceived[22] by the beneficiary is presented in Table 5.7. The table shows that at the national level, as much as 72 per cent of the sample beneficiaries thought that the asset they got was worth the cost. This percentage varied from 100 in Gujarat and Sikkim to as low as 8 in Manipur and Meghalaya. Thus, it can be said that barring a few exceptions, almost in all states, more than half of the IRDP beneficiaries thought that the assets they got were worth the price. In Gujarat and Sikkim, such was the view of all the beneficiaries.

Out of the remaining 28 per cent beneficiaries who thought that the cost of the asset was more than its value, 5 per cent reported that the excess cost was not more than Rs. 250, 5 per cent reported that it was between Rs. 251 and Rs. 500, 4 per cent reported that it was between Rs. 501 and Rs. 1000 and 14 per cent reported that it was more than Rs. 1000. Cases involving a difference of upto Rs. 250 varied

Table 5.7

Difference between Value and Cost of Asset

State	*Percentage in different ranges of Rupees*					
	0	*1-250*	*251-500*	*501-1000*	*>1000*	*Total*
Andhra Pradesh	88	3	4	2	3	100
Assam	43	11	12	14	20	100
Bihar	61	7	7	9	16	100
Gujarat	100	0	0	0	0	100
Haryana	58	4	18	9	11	100
Himachal Pradesh	90	4	2	1	3	100
Jammu & Kashmir	97	0	1	0	2	100
Karnataka	77	4	5	1	13	100
Kerala	60	27	10	0	3	100
Madhya Pradesh	58	7	8	5	22	100
Maharashtra	59	5	10	9	17	100
Manipur	8	1	11	6	74	100
Meghalaya	8	2	0	1	89	100
Nagaland	53	1	13	0	33	100
Orissa	77	5	5	8	5	100
Punjab	98	0	0	0	2	100
Rajasthan	72	2	1	0	25	100
Sikkim	100	0	0	0	0	100
Tamil Nadu	61	2	10	3	14	100
Tripura	97	1	0	0	2	100
Uttar Pradesh	92	3	3	1	1	100
West Bengal	96	3	0	0	1	100
Union Territories	86	4	5	2	3	100
National average	72	5	5	4	14	100

from nil in Gujarat, Jammu and Kashmir, Punjab and Sikkim to 27 per cent in Kerala. However, considering the fact that the average value of the asset was around Rs. 3000, even the upper limit of these differences, that is, Rs. 250 works out to only 8 per cent of the value of the asset. In view of the element of subjectivity involved in the estimates, a difference of this order can be treated as marginal. The differences of the order of Rs. 251 to Rs. 500 varied from nil in Gujarat, Meghalaya, Punjab, Sikkim, Tripura and West Bengal to 18 per cent in Haryana. Even differences upto Rs. 500 which work out to 16 per cent of the average cost of the asset can perhaps be considered tolerable in the light of the fact that excess demand for some of the popular IRDP assets led to price increases.[23] However, average differences of the order of more than Rs. 500 are cases needing closer attention and scrutiny. Together they accounted for 18 per cent of the sample beneficiaries at the national level. Cases where the differences are between Rs. 501 and Rs. 1,000 were below 10 per cent except in Assam where such cases accounted for 14 per cent of the total. The really alarming cases were the ones where differences were more than Rs. 1,000 which work out to more than one-third of the average cost of the asset. The national average of such cases from the sample was as high as 14 per cent. This means that out of the sixteen million and odd beneficiaries assisted during the period of survey, more than two million had to pay Rs. 1,000 or more as extra cost, or had to pay Rs. 3,000 for an asset worth less than Rs. 2,000. Such cases were as high as 89 per cent in Meghalaya and 74 per cent in Manipur. Other states where such cases are significant were Nagaland (33 per cent), Rajasthan (25 per cent), Madhya Pradesh (22 per cent) and Assam (20 per cent). This is a matter of serious concern.

It is well known that working capital[24] is an essential ingredient of some of the IRDP assets. In the absence of working capital, the asset will not be able to remain intact. Under such conditions, generating incremental income from such assets will be a far cry. From the data at our disposal, of all the sample beneficiaries, 34 per cent of them received working capital at the national level. About 40 per cent beneficiaries did not require any working capital. The remaining 25 per cent beneficiaries required working capital, but did not receive it. This is an aspect which needs to be looked into by the banks. The fact that nearly one-fourth of the total sample beneficiaries were not getting any working capital although they needed it, depicts the extremely callous attitude of the banks. This also indicates that followup of the beneficiaries by the banks is completely lacking. There was substantial variation in the provision of working capital across the states. The working capital was required but not provided in 78 per cent cases in Meghalaya, 70 per cent cases in Himachal Pradesh, 68 per cent cases in Jammu and Kashmir and 53 per cent cases in Maharashtra. Even in many other states, the percentages were quite high.

Status of the Asset

An important aspect of the IRDP is the durability of the asset which has been given to the beneficiary. This aspect requires serious consideration and has often been the subject of discussion and criticism. There are a number of issues involved. One, that the beneficiary has actually received the asset; second, that he is just the dejure owner of the asset. It is in this context that reference can be made to the 'Khutta baddaual' strategy[25] followed in certain areas. In a few cases, beneficiaries have also been given defective assets.[26] It is also argued that it is not possible for a poor beneficiary to maintain an asset given to him; sooner or later the asset has to be disposed off to meet unforeseen contingencies[27] the beneficiary faces. In fact, quite a number of instances have been reported by IRDP researchers and other observers which fall into one or the other of the above categories.

Table 5.8 gives the status of the asset. The table shows that at the national level, 72 per cent of the beneficiaries had the asset intact with them two years after the assistance, which is quite encouraging. The remaining 28 per cent cases where the assets were not intact comprised of cases where the assets were sold, fully perished, partly perished/defective and others, which included cases where the assets were not even purchased. Cases where a part of the asset had perished, had become defective or had been sold out were also included in 'not intact'

Table 5.8

Status of the Asset: Intact or Not Intact

State	*Per cent of the Beneficiaries*	
	Intact	*Not Intact*
Andhra Pradesh	74	26
Assam	70	30
Bihar	84	16
Gujarat	87	13
Haryana	44	56
Himachal Pradesh	85	15
Jammu & Kashmir	78	22
Karnataka	64	36
Kerala	73	27
Madhya Pradesh	72	28
Maharashtra	68	32
Manipur	32	68
Meghalya	32	68
Nagaland	69	31
Orissa	67	33
Punjab	77	23
Rajasthan	47	53
Sikkim	100	0
Tamil Nadu	62	28
Tripura	100	0
Uttar Pradesh	79	21
West Bengal	97	3
Union Territories	75	25
National average	72	28

cases. The statewise distribution of the assets indicated that in Sikkim all the assets were intact. On the contrary, in Manipur and Meghalaya, only 32 per cent of the assets were intact, which also means that as much as 68 per cent of the assets were either sold out, partially or fully perished. Other states where a high percentage of assets were not inact were Haryana (56 per cent), Rajasthan (53 per cent), Karnataka (36 per cent) and Orissa (33 per cent).

The reasons attributed for the assets not being intact were many and varied. In 24 per cent cases at the national level, the assets were not intact due to unexpected events like illness, deaths, etc.; in 20 per cent cases because the income generated by the assets was not enough; in 16 per cent cases due to the defective condition of the asset; in 6 per cent cases because of high maintenance cost of the asset; in 7 per cent cases because the cost of maintenance turned out to be higher than anticipated on account of rise in prices of the input required for maintenance of the asset and in 4 per cent cases though the maintenance cost was as anticipated, it could not be afforded by the beneficiary due to compulsive immediate household consumption requirements. In the remaining 23 per cent cases, beneficiaries had disposed off the assets because of other reasons. Inadequate income generation and high cost of maintenance are related reasons in as much as both relate to income from the asset, one in relation to the fixed capital cost of the asset and the other in relation to the working capital requirements. If adequate amount of working capital is not provided according to the requirement of an asset, the asset, sooner or later, is bound to remain not intact.

There is a divergent picture of the reasons for the asset not being intact across the states. Unexpected events were the principal cause of assets not being intact in 87 per cent cases in Mizoram, 56 per cent cases in Manipur and 50 per cent cases in Andaman and Nicobar Islands. Insufficient income generation resulted in the loss/sale of asset in 35 to 36 per cent cases in Punjab and Madhya Pradesh, 31 to 33 per cent in Lakshadweep and Kerala and 20 to 28 per cent cases in Maharashtra, Himachal Pradesh, Orissa, Uttar Pradesh, Bihar and Tamil Nadu. The assets were not intact because of high maintenance cost in 38 per cent cases in Pondicherry, 17 per cent cases in Tamil Nadu and 11 to 15 per cent cases in Andhra Pradesh, Himachal Pradesh, Punjab and Jammu and Kashmir. The assets were not intact because of some defects in the assets in 32 to 35 per cent cases in Andhra Pradesh, Lakshadweep, Meghalaya and Gujarat, 25 to 28 per cent cases in Bihar, Haryana, Andaman and Nicobar Islands and Tamil Nadu and 21 per cent cases in Kerala and Manipur. In 35 per cent cases in Rajasthan, 14 per cent cases in Jammu and Kashmir, and 11 per cent cases in Kerala, the beneficiaries had disposed off the assets because their maintenance cost turned out to be higher than anticipated on account of rise in prices of the inputs required for the maintenance of the assets. Although the cost of maintenance of assets was anticipated, compulsory immediate household consumption requirements had forced the beneficiaries to dispose off the assets in 22 per cent cases in Jammu and Kashmir, 19 per cent cases in Orissa and 10 to 11 per cent cases in Delhi. The assets were not intact because of other reasons in all cases in Nagaland and in more than 50 per cent cases in Delhi and Meghalaya. Other reasons could be a variety of miscellaneous reasons which may vary from family to family, but they also include cases where the assets were not even given to the beneficiary, or the asset was given but the purpose was not so much to keep the asset for generating income. Rather it was only intended to be disposed off to get the cash benefit of the subsidy.

Sufficiency of Assistance

The question of sufficiency of IRDP assistance is indeed complex and is required to be viewed from two angles. One, whether the assistance is sufficient from the point of view of the cost of the asset, and two, whether it is sufficient from the point of view of the viability of the venture for crossing the poverty line. If one were to take the objectives of the IRDP in its true spirit, sufficiency should be understood from the point of view of the long term objective of generation of incremental income from the asset.[28] The Concurrent Evaluation of IRDP survey shows that at the national level, 81 per cent beneficiaries found the assistance sufficient for acquiring the assets. In the remaining 19 per cent cases, the beneficiaries did not find the assistance sufficient for acquiring the asset. Of these, in 14 per cent cases, the beneficiaries met the balance money from their own resources and in the remaining 5 per cent cases, they met it by borrowings. In all cases in Nagaland, Sikkim and Tripura and in more than 95 per cent cases in West Bengal, Lakshadweep and Madhya Pradesh did the beneficiaries find the assistance sufficient. Such cases were also higher than the national average of 81 per cent in Orissa, Uttar Pradesh, Bihar and several other states. The use of own mony was prevalent in 56 per cent cases in Arunachal Pradesh, 45 per cent cases each in Dadra and Nagar Haveli and in Meghalaya. The use of borrowed money to meet the balance mony was made in 33 per cent cases each in Haryana and Delhi, 28 per cent cases in Chandigarh, and 10 to 15 per cent cases in Rajasthan, Pondicherry, Tamil Nadu, Kerala and Andhra Pradesh.

Sectoral Distribution of Assets

The IRDP is often at times referred to as a 'milch animal' programme and has been largely criticised on this count. Though detailed guidelines have been issued by the central government regarding the surveys that are to be conducted for assessing the viability of different schemes before the formation of family plans, cluster plans and block plans, in actual practice, the block machinery is rather weak and at best tries to achieve the objective of target fulfilment. In achieving this target, the government functionaries often provide easily manageable assets to the beneficiaries irrespective of their income-generating potential, even against the beneficiaries' choice in some cases. In extreme cases, hundreds of milch-animals are distributed in drought-affected areas and in other cases, dozens of sewing machines are distributed to different women beneficiaries from a single village. There was a case where a beneficiary has had years of training as a carpenter and yet he was given a goat, since that was the only option open to him. Such whimsical allocations are often at times noticed

Table 5.9

Sectoral Distribution of Assets

State	*Primary*					*Secondary*	*Tertiary*	*Total*
	Agricul-ture	*Irriga-tion*	*Milch animal*	*Animal husbandry other than milch animal*	*Total primary*			
Andhra Pradesh	12	17	8	9	46	5	49	100
Assam	18	0	7	20	45	5	50	100
Bihar	7	4	21	4	36	9	55	100
Gujarat	17	5	36	4	62	3	35	100
Haryana	3	0	43	17	63	9	28	100
Himachal Pradesh	12	0	32	13	57	15	28	100
Jammu & Kashmir	6	0	25	18	49	15	36	100
Karnataka	18	3	39	16	76	8	16	100
Kerala	4	1	34	7	46	5	49	100
Madhya Pradesh	13	1	14	2	30	8	62	100
Maharashtra	12	3	25	18	58	6	36	100

Manipur	36	0	2	32	70	3	27	100
Meghalaya	27	0	0	54	81	9	10	100
Nagaland	30	0	15	45	90	0	10	100
Orissa	7	4	2	5	18	18	64	100
Punjab	2	0	2	49	53	9	38	100
Rajasthan	5	1	18	16	40	12	48	100
Sikkim	70	0	22	8	100	0	0	100
Tamil Nadu	7	0	30	21	58	7	35	100
Tripura	11	0	5	18	34	6	60	100
Uttar Pradesh	8	4	22	8	42	9	49	100
West Bengal	12	4	5	6	27	19	54	100
Union Territories	4	2	39	16	61	2	37	100
National average	12	3	21	12	48	8	44	100

only because of, as pointed out above, target achievement, as if that was the single objective of the IRDP.

The sectoral allocation of assets provided to the beneficiaries as obtained in the sample is presented in Table 5.9. The table shows that at the national level, 48 per cent of the beneficiaries had assets in the primary sector as compared to 8 per cent in the secondary sector and 44 per cent in the tertiary sector. This distribution is much more even compared to the highly skewed distribution in favour of the primary sector in the early years of the Sixth Plan.[29] The table also shows that there is considerable variation in the intersectoral proportions across the states. Primary sector share varied from 100 per cent in Sikkim to 18 per cent in Orissa. The share of the secondary sector varied from 19 per cent in West Bengal to nil in Nagaland and Sikkim, and that in the tertiary sector, from 64 per cent in Orissa to nil in Sikkim. The inter-sectoral distribution across the states can hardly be explained on economic lines.[30] It is interesting to note that the more backward states like Orissa and Madhya Pradesh had a higher percentage of schemes from the tertiary sector, being 64 and 62, respectively, in contrast to the agriculturally prosperous states of Punjab and Haryana, which placed greater emphasis on the primary sector. The percentages of schemes in the primary sector in these two states were 63 and 53 respectively. The most popular sub-sector within the primary sector is the animal husbandry sector, accounting for 33 per cent of the total number of schemes in different sectors. As a component of the primary sector, it accounted for as much as 69 per cent of the schemes out of the primary sector schemes. The state percentages of animal husbandry schemes varied from 60 each in Haryana and Nagaland to 7 per cent in Orissa. There were four other states, namely Karnataka, Meghalaya, Punjab and Tamil Nadu, apart from the Union Territories where animal husbandry schemes accounted for more than 50 per cent of the schemes. Milch-animal scheme was the most important component of the animal husbandry schemes, accounting for 63 per cent of the total schemes in the animal husbandry sector, at the national level. The percentage of the milch animal schemes in the animal husbandry sector was more than 50 in almost all states, the highest being in Gujarat (90 per cent). Agriculture and irrigation sector did not appear to be popular in the IRDP, accounting for a mere 15 per cent of the total IRDP schemes, and 31 per cent of the schemes from the primary sector. Agriculture and irrigation are basically land-based activities and does not fall within the purview of the IRDP beneficiaries who are mostly landless. Another interesting fact revealed by the table is that agriculture seemed to be doing well under the IRDP in north-eastern states like Manipur and Sikkim and the agriculturally prosperous states like Punjab and Haryana were having a very small chunk of the IRDP assistance in the agricultural sector. The tertiary sector also had an edge over the primary sector in as many as nine different states as well as the Union Territories.

Role of the Banks in IRDP Financing

The IRD programme is financed partly by government grants and partly by bank credit. The Sixth Plan outlay for IRDP of Rs. 4,500 crore consisted of Rs. 1,500 crore of budgetary grants and Rs. 3,000 crore of bank credit. Thus, the share of the bank as well as the government in IRDP financing was in the ratio of 2:1 during the Sixth Plan. In the Seventh Plan, roughly the same ratio is being maintained. As a major financer of the programme, banks are thus expected to play a very important role in IRDP financing. It is, however, seldom argued that banks are at best a passive partner in the IRD programme. Unlike in the case of District Rural Development Agencies (DRDAs) and block offices, banks are not allotted financial and physical targets to be achieved in the IRD programme. Banks have to cater to the needs of several priority sectors and for IRDP it has to fulfil a 40 per cent lending target. Normally, however, banks prefer to achieve this target by lending to more credit worthy customers,[31] whose projects are financially more viable. Since the IRDP beneficiaries are very many,[32] the banks have to handle many lending cases, which at times becomes a cumbersome affair. The staffing pattern in the rural branches does not match with the amount of activities the bank has to perform. Moreover, the block officials, who are highly enthusiastic about securing bank loan for providing assistance to IRDP beneficiaries, are not of much help in ensuring repayment of the loan.[33] Thus, the paucity of time, shortage of manpower and indifference of the block machinery force the bankers to keep their involvement in the IRDP to the minimum.

Bank-wise distribution of the share of the IRDP loan provided to the sample beneficiaries is given in table 5.10. While commercial banks accounted for 68 per cent of the loan, the percentage of loan accounted by regional rural banks (RRBs) was 26 and that by the cooperative banks was 6. Among states, the share of commercial banks varied from 100 per cent in Sikkim to 3 per cent in Meghalaya. The share of RRBs varied from 66 per cent in Tripura to nil in the Union Territories and Sikkim. Commercial banks and RRBs, thus, accounted for 94 per cent of the total loan at the national level. These two banks are complementary to each other. Commercial banks are also helped by RRBs in remote rural areas where they are not able to extend their own services.

The share of cooperative banks in the IRDP loans was a mere 6 per cent at the national level. Across the states it varied from 18 per cent in Kerala to nil in Himachal Pradesh, Sikkim, Tripura and West Bengal. Cooperative banks were expected to fare well in areas which have strong cooperative stronghold, like Gujarat and Maharashtra. But in these two states, their share was a mere 4 and 7 per cent. A notable aspect of the cooperative involvement is that its share in the IRDP loan has been steadily declining over the years.[34] The pressure and controls that RBI and NABARD can apply on cooperative are fewer as compared to that on commercial banks and RRBs. The RRBs, in fact, have come up in a big way in solving the problem of rural credit, through IRDP assistance.[35]

According to the guidelines issued by the Reserve Bank of India, all IRDP loans should be medium term loans, that

Table 5.10

Bankwise Distribution of Loan

(Percentage share)

State	*Comml. Bank*	*Regional Rural Bank*	*Coop. Bank*	*Total*
Andhra Pradesh	77	20	3	100
Assam	61	36	3	100
Bihar	77	21	2	100
Gujarat	80	16	4	100
Haryana	72	25	3	100
Himachal Pradesh	90	10	0	100
Jammu and Kashmir	36	60	4	100
Karnataka	82	15	3	100
Kerala	68	13	18	100
Madhya Pradesh	56	38	6	100
Maharashtra	81	12	7	100
Manipur	17	8	0	0
Meghalaya	3	0	0	0
Nagaland	50	0	0	0
Orissa	58	30	12	100
Punjab	76	21	3	100
Rajasthan	51	37	12	100
Sikkim	100	0	0	100
Tamil Nadu	70	6	24	100
Tripura	34	66	0	100
Uttar Pradesh	52	36	12	100
West Bengal	75	25	0	100
Union Territories	98	0	2	100
National average	68	26	6	100

is, the repayment schedule for these loans should not be less than three years. Apart from that, in case of certain assets where there is a gestation period for the generation of income from these assets, there should be a certain grace period before the repayment is to begin. These two conditions are extremely important from the viewpoint to economic viability of the IRDP schemes. However, in adequate number of cases, the RBI guidelines are set aside and banks providing IRDP assistance give short term loans, where the repayment capacity is less than three years. In such cases, the beneficiaries are unable to repay such loans on time, as a result of which the bank has to suffer.[36] Table 5.11 presents the repayment schedule of loans by the beneficiaries. At the national level, 12 per cent cases were those with repayment schedule less than three years, 35 per cent cases where the repayment schedule was three years and 53 per cent cases where the repayment schedule was more than three years. That is, in 12 per cent cases of IRDP loans, the banking institutions had flouted the IRDP guidelines. The percentage of cases where the repayment schedule was less than three years varied from 70 in Sikkim to 27 in Tamil Nadu. The other states where this percentage was high was Andhra Pradesh and West Bengal (24 per cent each). There was a considerable variation across the states in cases where the repayment schedule is three years. The percentage of such cases was 60 in Kerala to nil in Meghalaya. The combined share of the short term loans and those where the term is exactly three years is also given in the table. At the national level, the percentage of such cases was 47, with large variations across the states. The percentage of such cases varied from 93 in Sikkim to nil in Meghalaya. The states where such cases were more than 50 per cent were Andhra Pradesh, Assam, Bihar, Kerala, Manipur, Orissa, Tamil Nadu, Uttar Pradesh and West Bengal. The percentage of cases where the repayment schedule is more than five years or where the loan guidelines issued by the RBI have been followed in 'letter and spirit' by the banks varied across the states, being 100 per cent in Meghalaya to 7 per cent in Sikkim. The states which had least flouted the RBI norms were Gujarat, Haryana, Himachal Pradesh, Jammu and Kashmir, Karnataka, Madhya Pradesh,

Table 5.11

Repayment Schedule

(Percentage share)

State	*Less than three years*	*Three years*	*Three years*	*More than three years*	*Total*
Andhra Pradesh	24	42	66	34	100
Assam	15	45	60	40	100
Bihar	5	47	52	48	100
Gujarat	6	24	30	70	100
Haryana	12	14	26	74	100
Himachal Pradesh	7	33	40	60	100
Jammu and Kashmir	8	28	36	64	100
Karnataka	15	13	28	72	100
Kerala	12	60	72	28	100
Madhya Pradesh	7	38	45	55	100
Maharashtra	13	25	38	62	100
Manipur	0	52	52	48	100
Meghalaya	0	0	0	100	100
Nagaland	0	35	35	65	100
Orissa	18	51	69	31	100
Punjab	9	35	44	56	100
Rajasthan	9	15	24	76	100
Sikkim	70	23	93	7	100
Tamil Nadu	27	37	64	36	100
Tripura	1	42	43	57	100
Uttar Pradesh	12	52	64	36	100
West Bengal	24	45	69	31	100
Union Territories	14	32	46	54	100
National average	12	35	47	53	100

Table 5.12

Amount of Overdues

(Percentage in different ranges in Rs.)

State	*0*	*1-250*	*251-1,000*	*1,001-2,000*	*>2,000*	*Total*
Andhra Pradesh	42	12	27	14	5	100
Assam	9	5	35	32	19	100
Bihar	24	6	30	27	13	100
Gujarat	49	3	28	13	7	100
Haryana	27	2	19	27	25	100
Himachal Pradesh	59	6	20	8	7	100
Jammu and Kashmir	58	6	14	9	13	100
Karnataka	36	6	26	25	7	100
Kerala	27	17	32	17	7	100
Madhya Pradesh	32	7	30	25	6	100
Maharashtra	43	9	25	17	6	100
Manipur	73	0	2	21	4	100
Meghalaya	100	0	0	0	0	100
Nagaland	100	0	0	0	0	100
Orissa	32	13	37	16	3	100
Punjab	71	1	9	15	4	100
Rajasthan	33	10	32	18	7	100
Sikkim	30	0	19	26	25	100
Tamil Nadu	43	10	19	16	12	100
Tripura	15	15	45	17	8	100
Uttar Pradesh	52	74	18	17	9	100
West Bengal	26	12	38	13	11	100
Union Territories	42	7	16	21	14	100
National average	42	6	25	18	9	100

Table 5.13

Reasons for Overdues

(Percentages)

State	Inadequate income	Unforeseen calamity	Tight repayment schedule	Others	Tota
Andhra Pradesh	41	22	33	4	100
Assam	72	3	25	0	100
Bihar	55	4	41	0	100
Gujarat	45	12	40	3	100
Haryana	40	0	60	0	100
Himachal Pradesh	53	8	36	3	100
Jammu and Kashmir	70	10	18	2	100
Karnataka	63	2	30	5	100
Kerala	65	10	32	3	100
Madhya Pradesh	56	3	40	1	100
Maharashtra	72	4	23	1	100
Manipur	28	54	18	0	100
Meghalaya	—	—	—	—	—
Nagaland	—	—	—	—	—
Orissa	54	8	28	0	100
Punjab	66	11	21	2	100
Rajasthan	38	30	10	22	100
Sikkim	100	0	0	0	100
Tamil Nadu	64	4	31	1	100
Tripura	40	5	55	0	100
Uttar Pradesh	51	13	35	1	100
West Bengal	47	10	34	9	100
Union Territories	38	12	48	2	100
Nationai average	54	10	33	3	100

Maharashtra, Nagaland, Punjab, Rajasthan, Tripura and the Union Territories.

One of the important criticisms which is often raised against the beneficiaries of the IRDP is that they do not repay the loans on time. In some cases, the repayments are not made deliberately,[37] although such cases are scanty. This is a valid concern especially for the banks, which has had a very sad experience in the past, as far as repayment is concerned in other priority lending areas. The banking industry may stop functioning if substantial portions of bank finances are tied up with the borrowers as overdues. Table 5.12 gives a review of the overdues position of IRDP loans. The table shows that 42 per cent of the beneficiaries had no overdues at the national level. The percentage of such cases varied from 100 each in Meghalaya and Nagaland to 9 in Assam. The achievement of Meghalaya and Nagaland can be considered to be commendable. Six per cent of the beneficiaries had an amount of overdues of upto Rs. 250 only at the national level, which again will be considered a marginal overdue. It can be inferred that 48 per cent of the beneficiaries at the national level were non-defaulters, which should be considered to be a happy situation both from the view of the bank as well as the government machinery.[38] Out of the remaining 52 per cent of cases, 25 per cent had overdues between Rs. 251 and Rs. 1,000, 18 per cent had overdues between Rs. 1,001 and Rs. 2,000 and the rest 9 per cent had overdues beyond Rs. 2,000.[39] The state percentages in the category of Rs. 251-1000 varied from 45 in Tripura to nil in Meghalaya and Nagaland. The state percentages in the immediate next category of Rs. 1,001-2,000 varied from 32 in Assam to nil in Meghalaya and Nagaland. Similarly, the share of beneficiaries with overdues more than Rs. 2,000 varied from 25 per cent each in Haryana and Sikkim to nil in Meghalaya and Nagaland.

Although the percentage of overall overdues is not that alarming, it is the overdues in the category of Rs. 1,001-2,000 that should catch the attention of planners of the IRDP schemes. Several reasons could be adduced to non-repayment of loans. Some of the overdues may be due to the unrealistic repayment schedule.[40] Others may be due to the non-viability of the scheme in a particular area.[41] There may be other cases where the asset provided was not issued and subsequently perished due to accident or death. There may be still other cases where the beneficiaries were wilful defaulters. Unless these factors are identified, banks' association with the IRD programme will at best be half-hearted. To check this deficiency in the functioning of IRDP, it is necessary to identify the reasons for non-payment of loan on time.

Table 5.13 gives the reasons for overdues among the sample beneficiaries. 54 per cent of them reported that inadequate income generation from the given asset was the main reason for overdues. Tight repayment schedule was the reason next in importance which accounted for 33 per cent of the cases of overdues.[42] Unforeseen calamities[43] accounted for 10 per cent of the cases of overdues and other reasons accounted for 3 per cent of the overdue cases. Other reasons generally refer to deliberate default on the part of the beneficiaries. There are, however, wide variations across the states so far as reasons for overdues are concerned. In Sikkim, 100 per cent of the beneficiaries reported inadequate income on the one hand, to 28 per cent in Manipur, on the other. Unforeseen calamities accounted for 54 per cent of the beneficiaries in Manipur to nil in Haryana and Sikkim. Similarly, tight repayment schedule was the main reason for 60 per cent of the beneficiaries in Haryana to nil in Sikkim. Other reasons accounted for 22 per cent of the overdue cases in Rajasthan. The next highest percentage of cases accounting for this reason was 9 in West Bengal to 5 or less in all other states. This fact needs to be probed into as it has an important bearing on policy implications.

Horizontal and Vertical Linkages

The Sixth Plan has specifically stated that for the successful implementation of IRDP, it would be necessary to establish adequate horizontal linkages with a number of other programmes at that field level. The Seventh Plan has since again reiterated, for example, that IRDP and employment programmes are not mutually exclusive. Employment programmes provided secure wage-income to the poor through the creation of durable community assets. In fact, the Plan document has even noted that the total impact of IRDP depends on the degree to which the different poverty alleviation programmes —NREP or RLEGP are integrated with one another and with overall development of the area. The other programmes would include TRYSEM and DWCRA. With a concern for the above relationship and interlinkages of IRDP, the concurrent evaluation has attempted to find out the number of cases in which any member of IRDP gets benefit of the other programmes like NREP/RLEGP and TRYSEM/DWCRA. Table 5.14 makes a review of the benefits of employment the IRDP beneficiaries or members of their family have received under the different programmes. The table reveals that only in 10 per cent cases at the national level such benefits were obtained under NREP/ RLEGP and in 4 per cent cases under TRYSEM/DWCRA. This shows that the linkages of IRDP with the other programmes are very poor. At the states' level, such benefits were obtained from 100 per cent in Sikkim under NREP/RLEGP to nil in Manipur and Nagaland. Similar was the case under TRYSEM/ DWCRA, where 100 per cent benefits were obtained in Sikkim to nil in Bihar, Karnataka, Meghalaya, Nagaland, Rajasthan, Tamil Nadu and Tripura. The example of Sikkim needs to be highlighted. This state is a glaring example of horizontal linkage. If self-employment and wage-employment are so closely linked, IRDP will be able to bear extremely fruitful results. Other states should try to emulate the example of Sikkim.

The reasons for inadequate programme linkage could be many and varied. The first is that the block machinery in itself is not adequate to generate a beneficial working relationship between the beneficiaries and other programmes of employment generation. It is because of the fact that the intersectoral linkages at the block level are found to be lacking.[44] There could also be problems of coordination which inhibit an overall harmonious outreach effort to mobilise the beneficiary at the local level.[45] Inadequate dissemination about what other programmes are concurrently offering can also be a probable cause. Whatever the reasons, the concurrent evaluation clearly underlines the need for strengthening the linkages of IRDP with other related programmes. The linkages, as of now, are limited, due to the weakness of the administrative set-up at the local level and the lack of support of sectoral and subject-matter specialists at the state level.

Table 5.14

Employmeat Under Other Programmes

State	*Percentage of beneficiaries/ family members*	
	NREP/RLEGP	*TRYSEM/DWCRA*
Andhra Pradesh	7	2
Assam	2	4
Bihar	7	0
Gujarat	12	2
Haryana	35	7
Himachal Pradesh	2	9
Jammu and Kashmir	10	9
Karnataka	10	0
Kerala	7	3
Madhya Pradesh	9	1
Maharashtra	6	3
Manipur	0	3
Meghalaya	15	0
Nagaland	0	0
Orissa	2	1
Punjab	3	11
Rajasthan	15	0
Sikkim	100	100
Tamil Nadu	3	0
Tripura	43	0
Uttar Pradesh	6	3
West Bengal	42	24
Union Territories	20	6
National average	10	4

Vertical linkages refer to the linkages within the IRD programme, both backward and forward. The absence of such linkages has been a subject of vehement criticism in several IRDP studies which conclude that the absence of such linkages has been largely responsible for the failure of IRDP. The presence/absence of backward and forward linkages is reflected from the adequacy/inadequacy of existing infrastructure[46] available with the sample beneficiaries. The adequacy of existing

Table 5.15

Adequacy of Existing Infrastructure

(*Percentage of beneficiaries*)

State	*Inputs*	*Marketing*	*Repair*
Andhra Pradesh	2	10	8
Assam	4	9	0
Bihar	1	2	0
Gujarat	3	4	36
Haryana	6	17	5
Himachal Pradesh	10	0	93
Jammu and Kashmir	10	4	23
Karnataka	1	15	1
Kerala	3	28	1
Madhya Pradesh	2	18	0
Maharashtra	4	15	7
Manipur	5	1	7
Meghalaya	0	8	2
Orissa	2	16	1
Punjab	12	22	2
Rajasthan	1	12	0
Sikkim	100	98	0
Tamil Nadu	1	19	30
Tripura	0	0	0
Uttar Pradesh	4	7	1
West Bengal	23	0	0
Union Territories	8	2	16
National average	4	14	5

infrastructure has been given in Table 5.15. It is clear from the table that the existing infrastructure available to the IRDP beneficiaries is extremely inadequate. At the national level, inputs were available only to 4 per cent of the beneficiaries, marketing facilities to 14 per cent and repair facilities to only 5 per cent of the beneficiaries. The achievement of Sikkim once again is commendable. In this state, all IRDP beneficiaries had access to input and marketing facilities. The percentage of beneficiaries having facilities of repair service in this state was nil, which could also mean that none of the assets in Sikkim needed repair, which, however, is quite unlikely. The percentage of beneficiaries having facilities of input availability was 10 or below in all states except West Bengal where this percentage was 23. Repair facilities were available to 93 per cent of the beneficiary in Himachal Pradesh, which gives an indication of the high degree of repair of assets required in this state. Provision of adequate infrastructural facilities and on time is one of the basic requirement of the IRDP asset if it is to fulfil its objective of income generation. In the absence of such facilities, all IRDP efforts to alleviate poverty are bound to be a futile exercise.

After Care Support

The beneficiaries provided with income generating assets require support and assistance on a continuing basis. Since the beneficiaries are well below the poverty line, they are victims of other disabilities as well which makes them vulnerable and helpless before the socio-economic forces working against their upliftment. However, support provided by the government machinery does not appear to be adequate as reflected from several evaluation studies. In this context, the concurrent evaluation figures are in consonance with the results of earlier studies, which is evident from Table 5.16. The table reveals that only 21 per cent of the beneficiaries received after care support by the government at the national level. The percentage of beneficiaries not receiving any after care support from the government was as high as 57 at the national level. The rest 22 per cent of the beneficiaries did not require any

Table 5.16

After Care Support by Government

(Percentage of beneficiaries)

State	*Yes*	*No*	*Not required*	*Total*
Andhra Pradesh	27	30	43	100
Assam	7	83	10	100
Bihar	11	74	15	100
Gujarat	33	57	67	100
Haryana	32	21	47	100
Himachal Pradesh	74	3	23	100
Jammu and Kashmir	18	71	11	100
Karnataka	26	53	21	100
Kerala	8	80	2	100
Madhya Pradesh	12	17	71	100
Maharashtra	28	70	2	100
Manipur	16	79	5	100
Meghalaya	2	97	1	100
Nagaland	100	0	0	100
Orissa	61	38	1	100
Punjab	43	57	0	100
Rajasthan	4	83	13	100
Sikkim	100	0	0	100
Tamil Nadu	39	59	3	100
Tripura	99	0	1	100
Uttar Pradesh	6	55	39	100
West Bengal	100	0	0	100
Union Territories	28	15	57	100
National average	21	57	22	100

after care support. In between the states, in Nagaland, Sikkim and West Bengal, all the beneficiaries received after care support by the government, for which the government machinery in these states deserves all praise. On the contrary in Meghalaya, Rajasthan, Uttar Pradesh and Assam, the percentage of beneficiaries receiving after care support from the government was as low as 2, 3, 6 and 7 respectively. If we compare Meghalaya and Nagaland, the two north eastern states, it is interesting to see the attitude of the government towards the IRD programmes; one, where the percentage is 2, is of extreme indifference and callousness, and the other, where the percentage is 100 is of utmost sincerity and concern. In between these two extremes are several states where the percentage ranges between 30 and 70.

These figures pose questions to all those concerned with the implementation of IRDP in general and to the local level functionaries in particular. It also raises some pertinent issues. Is it realised that in the existing situation when there is no organisation of beneficiaries, government is alone in a position to provide support and care ? Is the VLW capable of providing support and care, constrained as he is by his own limited skills and the overstretched meagre administrative resources at his command? These are some of the issues which need to be probed into in detail. It also seems that realising the constraints, beneficiaries tend to adopt a withdrawal approach in the post-asset transfer situation. This is not difficult to comprehend because of the fragile resource base of the rural poor and his almost negligible access to additional inputs. The need for continuing support and care is thus imperative to arrest the withdrawal approach, or else the household will again disappear in the mass of the poorest poor.[47]

It is in this context that reference should be made of the organisation of beneficiaries and to other organisations looking after the interests of the beneficiaries. The concurrent evaluation shows that the organisation of beneficiaries was working only in 9 per cent cases at the national level. In the remaining 91 per cent cases, there was no organisation of the beneficiaries. Across the states there was a divergent picture. Such organisations were working in 30 per cent cases in Madhya Pradesh, 20 per cent cases in Pondicherry, 13 per cent cases in Tamil Nadu, 9 per cent cases in Andhra Pradesh, 7 per cent cases in Gujarat and 6 per cent cases each in Meghalaya and Uttar

Pradesh. Such organisations were also found in less than 5 per cent cases in Karnataka, Maharashtra, Andaman and Nicobar Islands, Rajasthan, West Bengal, Kerala, Assam, Bihar, Jammu and Kashmir and Punjab. In other states, however, such organisations were not working. In those cases where no organisation of beneficiaries was working, it was ascertained whether any other organisation was working there to look after the interest of the beneficiary. It is observed that other organisations were looking after the interest of the beneficiaries in 5 per cent cases at the national level. Such organisations were looking after beneficiaries' interests in all cases in Nagaland and 88 per cent cases in Meghalaya. They were also working in 22 per cent cases in West Bengal and in less than 20 per cent cases in several states. In Bihar, Haryana, Manipur, Orissa, Punjab, Rajasthan, Sikkim, Tripura and in the Union Territories, such organisations were not working.

Training in Handling of Assets

Many critics have called IRDP a programme of loan disbursement by the banks. This narrow objective of IRDP perceived by the banks has, in fact, been responsible for its failure. Criticism on this count appears just in the sense that there is no followup on the IRDP either by the banks or by the government machinery and bank's role has actually been limited, in practice, to the disbursement of loans. The question of training in IRDP is indeed complex. The beneficiary, illiterate and unaware that he is, does not actually know whether the asset provided to him requires training or not. He perceives training in his own narrow sense. Either he is totally unaware of the expected productive potential of the asset or he prefers to rely on age old methods handed over to him as a tradition. Under such conditions, he would not expect any type of training for handling the asset.[48] The vicious cycle of presumed knowledge in handling the assets has to be broken, or else in spite of IRDP intervention, bulk of the rural poor will be forever struggling to cross the level of poverty to which they have been clinging for years together.

Table 5.17

Training in Handling of Assets

(Percentage of beneficiaries)

State	*Given*	*Not given*	*Not required*	*Total*
Andhra Pradesh	2	16	82	100
Assam	3	31	66	100
Bihar	1	43	56	100
Gujarat	2	32	66	100
Haryana	2	12	86	100
Himachal Pradesh	6	13	81	100
Jammu and Kashmir	0	45	55	100
Karnataka	3	27	70	100
Kerala	16	32	52	100
Madhya Pradesh	2	21	77	100
Maharashtra	4	58	38	100
Manipur	2	62	36	100
Meghalaya	1	19	80	100
Nagaland	8	58	36	100
Orissa	7	29	64	100
Punjab	1	0	99	100
Rajasthan	0	43	97	100
Sikkim	0	13	87	100
Tamil Nadu	1	7	92	100
Tripura	0	100	0	100
Uttar Pradesh	3	11	86	100
West Bengal	6	57	37	100
Union Territories	3	10	87	100
National average	3	29	68	100

According to the concurrent evaluation, in about 68 per cent cases, the beneficiaries did not require any training in the handling of assets (Table 5.17). This speaks clearly of their perception of training. In about 32 per cent cases, training was required by the beneficiaries, but it was not imparted to them in 29 per cent cases. The actual training was given to the beneficiaries only in the remaining 3 per cent cases. In between states, the highest percentage of training was imparted in Kerala (16 per cent) to nil in Jammu and Kashmir, Rajasthan, Sikkim and Tripura. Of these states, training was not given to a single beneficiary in Tripura, all of whom required training and 45 per cent of the beneficiaries in Jammu and Kashmir who required training. In as many as ten states, more than 80 per cent of the beneficiaries felt that they did not require any training in the handling of assets.

Closely related to the question of training is the provision of Vikas Patrika,[49] which is an important component of the followup aspect of IRDP. It has been prescribed under the IRDP for regularly monitoring the annual income of the beneficiary and the status of the asset provided to him. The Vikas Patrika is provided to the beneficiary at the time of his selection and checked and updated by the block officials. The distribution of the cases where Vikas Patrika was provided to the beneficiaries and the cases where it was updated has been recorded in the concurrent evaluation. It is observed that Vikas Patrika was provided to the beneficiaries in about 31 per cent cases at the national level. Of these, it was updated only in 19 per cent cases. This shows the negligence of the followup aspect of IRDP by the concerned authorities. Across the states, Vikas Patrika was distributed in 75 per cent cases each in Kerala and Lakshadweep to 2-4 per cent cases in Haryana and Maharashtra.

Notes and References

1. Kurien, N.J., "IRDP: how relevant is it ?", Economic and Political Weekly, Vol. XXII, No. 52, Dec. 26, 1987, p. A-161.

2. The identification of the poor is based on a modestly defined poverty line to ensure a consumption basket which includes the minimum calorie requirements. The poverty line is usually measured as the mid-point of the frequency class interval of National Sample Survey Consumer expenditure estimates, which contains the minimum calorie requirements.

3. The target for the Seventh Plan is fixed at 20 million beneficiaries. The total amount allocated including bank credit is about Rs. 7,000 crores.

4. Subbarao, K., "Regional variations in the impact of anti-poverty programme: a review of evidence", Economic and Political Weekly, Oct. 26, 1985.

5. The Concurrent Evaluation Survey of IRDP was carried out by reputed research institutions in the country on behalf of the Department of Rural Development, Ministry of Agriculture, Government of India during January to December 1987.

6. The debate was initiated by Rath in his article, "Garibi Hatao: can IRDP do it ?", Economic and Political Weekly, Feb. 9, 1985, which was followed by a discussion on Rath's paper by Hirway, Economic and Political Weekly, March 30, 1985. Subbarao's article, Economic and Political Weekly, Oct. 26, 1985, contributes a lot to this debate. In this connection, also see Guhan, S., "Reaching out to the poor", Economic Times, Silver Jubilee Special, Dec. 19, 1986 and "Rural poverty: policy and play acting", Economic and Political Weekly, Nov. 2, 1980. Also see Bagchee Sandip, "Poverty alleviation programmes in the Seventh Plan: an appraisal", Economic and Political Weekly, Jan. 24, 1987; Dantwala, M.L., "Garibi hatao : strategy options", Economic and Political Weekly, March 16, 1985; Kanakalata, Mukund, "Bank credit and IRDP, Madhya Pradesh experience", Economic and Political Weekly, Oct. 11, 1986; Kurien, N.J., op. cit. (1).

7. The more important evaluation studies are the ones by (1) Programme Evaluation Organisation (PEO) of the Planning Commission, which covered 16 states, 33 districts, 66 blocks and 1,179 households and was released in May 1985, (2) Reserve Bank of India (RBI) which covered 16 districts in 16 states, (3) National Bank for Agriculture and Rural Development (NABARD), which covered 30 districts and 60 blocks in 16 states, and (4) Institute for Financial Management and Research (IFMR), which covered 17 blocks, and 5 districts in 3 states. The IFMR sample size in terms of beneficiary families was 1857 besides a cont roup of 1007 non-beneficiary families.

8. Op. cit. (I), p. A-162.

9. The cut off point, however, was Rs. 4,800 and it was decided that families would be first brought from the level of Rs. 3,500 to Rs. 4800 and subsequently to Rs. 6,400.

10. This refers to the PEO, RBI, NABARD and IFMR studies.

11. By the time the beneficiaries in the sample were assisted, the poverty line, adjusted for inflation, had actually crossed the Rs. 6,000 mark. As such Rs. 4,800 as cut off, is, in effect, a conservative criterion.

12. Kurien points out that the very mechanical criterion of 3,000 beneficiaries per block throughout the country created problems of selection of enough number of eligible beneficiaries in Punjab or elsewhere. For example, in north-eastern states and the hill tracts of Himachal Pradesh, Jammu and Kashmir and Uttar Pradesh, there are blocks with less than 3,00 families let alone families which are below the poverty line, or which are in the category of 'destitutes' or 'very very poor'.

13. Gram sabha is the traditional village assembly in which all the adult members of the village can attend and deliberate on matters concerning the whole community or its members. This institution is a common heritage in most parts of the country. The significant exceptions are Kerala and Tamil Nadu where villages are usually much bigger than elsewhere and as such the general assembly of the village may become too crowded.

14. This finding corroborates the finding of an earlier study undertaken by Kurien.

15. Saxena, A.P., "Concurrent evaluation of IRDP: selected aspects for administrative followup", Economic and Political Weekly, Sept. 26, 1987, p. A-121.

16. Ibid., p. A-122.

17. There is no provision for recording such cases of corruption in the main body of the schedule. The content analyses of the remarks column of the schedule (in which such cases are mentioned as examples of corruption) have not been given in the main findings of the concurrent evaluation of IRDP survey to enable us record such cases, which would have been there in the schedules not canvassed by us.

18. It is very difficult to seek information from a particular beneficiary about bribe payments. Normally, when an investigator interviews a beneficiary, some influential person from the village or the VLW is always by his side, and such situations are difficult to avoid.

Under such circumstances, even if a beneficiary wants to confide with the investigator with regard to bribe payment, he is reluctant to do so. In some of the areas, for example, in Bihar, such malpractices have become almost institutionalised, as a result of which a certain percentage of the share from the beneficiary has been fixed for the implementing authorities, which a beneficiary, as a rule, has to part with. Specific examples are difficult to cite. There is an interesting strategy of 'Khutta baddaual', in which the same cow is sold several times in the market and is tied in the house of different beneficiaries at different points of time. Such cases of malpractices can take place only by the beneficiaries' connivance with the authorities.

19. It is being realised, however, that the purchase committee does not cater to the interests of a beneficiary, but in turn, exploits him. Under such conditions, an idea was passed that the purchase committee be abolished and that loans be given to the beneficiaries in cash rather than in kind. In fact, such a change has been introduced in certain blocks, and the results are awaited. There is an apprehension, however, that the assets might not be purchased at all, and the money given in the form of loan might be used for some other purpose, like the performance of a marriage or meeting other rituals. Under such situations, the possibility of which cannot be ruled out, the entire purpose of the IRDP will be defeated. The best economic use of money (whether it be in the form of subsidy or loan) to a beneficiary will not necessarily be the same as that envisaged in the IRDP.

20. It is customary, almost invariably,that apart from the direct benefits accruing to the important officials on the basis of a pre-determined formula, even fringe benefits like a 'nashta' (snacks and tea), would be extracted by the officials from the beneficiary.

21. Since there is no procurement price of the asset, IRDP price generally tends to be higher than the market price. IRDP assets under such conditions become 'premium products', as Kurien terms it.

22. Since the question of perception of the beneficiary is involved here, there is a high element of subjectivity in his answer. The results are, nevertheless, significant, as they throw light on the relative 'mark up' across the states.

23. The typical examples of such assets are milch animals, sheep, goat, bullock, etc., for which the short-term supply elasticity is comparatively low.

24. Working capital can be defined as the capital required to make the asset function properly in order to reap economic benefits. The

working capital for an asset like a cow, for example, would be the money required on its feed and fodder and expenses incurred on its regular health checkup. If the cow is not given proper diet and if it is unhealthy, it will not be able to give quality milk and in adequate quantity. However, there are a number of assets which do not require working capital.

25. See the note no. 18 for a description of this strategy. It is in this context that the IRDP cow has been called a 'circulating capital' by Dandekar.
26. A sick cow, for example, can be referred to as a defective asset.
27. These unforeseen contingencies can be in the form of a death of a relative, marriage in the family, repair of house, etc. IRDP funds are often at times diverted to meet these contingencies.
28. It is my firm belief that no beneficiary would view sufficiency from the angle of income generation. The beneficiaries' perception in this connection remains confined to the short term requirement.
29. Though there were no fixed targets in terms of percentage shares for different sectors during the Sixth Plan, the guidelines indicated that the desired distribution is two-thirds for primary sector and one-third share for the other two sectors to be shared equally. However, in actual practice the primary sector accounted for 94 per cent in 1980-81 and 83 per cent in 1981-82. This percentage came down to 55 by 1984-85.
30. Thus, the rationale of target-fulfilment approach gains further ground.
31. A bank, by definition, is an institution which provides loans to individuals who deal in ventures which have economic viability. The credit worthiness of an individual is judged by his capacity to repay the loan on time so that the institution of banking also derives some economic gain in the process.
32. Six hundred beneficiaries have to be given financial assistance through the IRDP scheme from every block every year.
33. Such a loan is, by and large, considered to be a bad loan by the banks, which makes them reluctant in granting such loans to the IRDP beneficiaries.
34. The share of cooperatives has steadily come down from 37 per cent in 1980-81 to 10 per cent in 1984-85.
35. Mohsin, Nadeem and R. Jha, "Regional rural banks and IRDP", Yojana, Vol. 31, No. 13, July 16-31, 1987.
36. The problem of untimely repayment is as much the fault of the beneficiary as it is of the bank. If banks providing IRDP assis-

tance were to strictly follow the RBI guidelines, repayment would have been more smooth and timely.

37. A very interesting example is from the district of Nawadah in Bihar, where beneficiaries have been given to learn that loans have not to be repaid at all, and the banks under no circumstance will be questioning about the repayment.

38. At what cost loans are being repaid is a situation that needs to be closely monitored. Many beneficiaries sell off the assets to repay the loan, which goes against the basic objective of IRDP.

39. The amount of Rs. 2,000 and above is an exhorbitant amount of overdue considering that the average amount of IRDP loan per beneficiary is about Rs. 2,000. These are the cases where no amount of loan has ever been repaid, or whatever little has been repaid is too meagre to be considered a repayment.

40. Repayment schedule, as a matter of fact, should vary from scheme to scheme and even should be in certain ways linked to the pre-assistance income of the beneficiaries. Schemes with shorter gestation periods start generating income faster than schemes with longer gestation periods. Apart from that, beneficiaries with lower pre-assistance incomes (destitutes and very very poor) are likely to eat up the entire lot of whatever little income is generated from the scheme at least in the initial phase of the programme, and so would be unlikely making regular loan repayments.

41. For the economic viability of a scheme in a particular area, care should be taken of the necessary linkages, both backwards and forwards, like provision of inputs and necessary infrastructure like transportation, marketing, etc., to make the output from the scheme saleable at an attractive price.

42. Inadequate income generation and tight repayment schedule are interrelated reasons in a sense that a repayment schedule which does not match with the income generation capacity of the scheme is bound to cause overdues, in spite of the best intentions of the beneficiary.

43. Refer note 27. It also includes in this survey defective assets or assets not intact.

44. This observation was made in the Report of the Committee to review the existing administrative arrangements for rural development and poverty alleviation programmes, Department of Rural Development, Ministry of Agriculture, 1985.

45. Saxena, A.P., "Coordination factor in regional development", *in* 'Institutional Dimensions of Regional Development', United Nations Centre for Regional Development, Nagoya, 1981.

46. Although infrastructure has a wider connotation, in the context of the concurrent evaluation of the IRDP survey, it refers to the availability of inputs to the beneficiaries, the extent of marketing facilities available to them and the provision for repair of assets if and when necessary. For example, if the asset happened to be a milch cow, the inputs required would be feed and fodder and veterinary service for regular health check ups. Similarly, marketing would mean the marketing of milk produced by the cow in order to ensure the best price, and repair would refer to the provision for medicines for cure from various diseases. Thus, there would be a similar infrastructure for each and every scheme.
47. Op. cit. (15), p. A-123.
48. A beneficiary might feel that he does not require any type of training for handling the asset; it is the job of the bank to impart training and convince the beneficiary that training for him is absolutely essential to make the asset perform the best.
49. Vikas Patrika is a booklet meant for the beneficiaries. It contains information related to beneficiary's identification, his asset, etc. It is divided into seven sections. Section I contains generel information about the identification of the beneficiary. Section II contains information regarding his socio-economic status and other information to find him suitable for being trained. Section III contains information about the trained beneficiaries. It goes into specific details about the type of training imparted and also the place and duration of training. Section IV deals with the financial assistance provided to the beneficiary. It contains information about the amount of loan sanctioned as well as disbursed, the specific date on which the disbursement took place, the rate of interest on the loan, the actual number of instalments on which the loan amount is to be repaid, and the actual date from which the repayment begins. It also provides information about the bank which gives loan, the date of forward of loan application from the block to the bank, etc. Section V contains information about the other types of assistance provided to the beneficiary like the supply of raw materials for the assets, the existing market conditions, other bottlenecks in the implementation of the scheme and their possible remedies, etc. Section VI contains information about the income generated from the scheme at the end of the first year, after two years and in the years following. Section VII contains information about the dates of visits of the field supervisors/inspectors to assist the beneficiaries, the action taken by them thereafter and their remarks on the performance of the beneficiaries.

6

Crossing the Poverty Barrier

The single criterion of 'crossing the poverty line', to judge the performance of IRDP has been a subject of criticism[1], although the four important studies on IRDP, a mention of which has been made in an earlier chapter, have all followed this sole criterion for evaluating the performance of IRDP. This poverty line criterion so strictly adhered to has been largely responsible for an almost universal view of the failure of IRDP. Even researchers like Rath have had this narrow view and have been forced to make dramatic conclusions about the results of IRDP.[2] An asset might prove to be highly productive and generate adequate income under certain circumstance, while under others it might prove to be the greatest liability. This would depend broadly upon two factors : the status of the recipient of the asset and the infrastructural facilities in terms of linkages available to the beneficiary. For example, a beneficiary belonging to a destitute or very very poor category would not be able to extract as much from an asset as would a beneficiary belonging to the poor or not so poor category. If these categories were represented in terms of their annual family income, the higher the income of the beneficiary, the greater would be his chances of crossing the poverty line within a specified time span. On the contrary, the lower the income of the beneficiary, the lesser would be his chances of crossing the poverty line. Lower pre-assistance income categories generally tend to absorb the meagre incremental IRDP gains in areas which are non-productive rather than re-investing them completely on the asset, as a result of which the asset given to such categories is not able to generate an income adequate enough to raise them above the poverty line within a specified time span. Even if the incremental capital-output ratio (ICOR) of the asset owned by a beneficiary with a very low pre-assistance income is the same as that owned by a beneficiary with a pre-assistance income on the brink of the poverty line income, the latter is likely to cross the poverty line within a specified time span, although the former has derived equal economic gains (in terms of incremental income), since the ICOR of the assets belonging to the two categories are equal,[3] whereas their pre-assistance incomes are different.

There is no denying the fact that the poorer a beneficiary, the lesser does he have access to infrastructural facilities in terms of procurement of inputs, marketing, etc.[4] With a weak linkage and an already weak economic base, such beneficiaries generally tend to opt for assets which involve smaller outlays and hence give lower returns. Assets with land-based activities owned, for example, by small farmers[5] who prefer pump-sets/tubewells, etc., involve larger outlays.[6] If we were to scan through the allotment of schemes in the present survey, we would find that the assets, by and large, have been according to the choice of the beneficiary, although the beneficiary's choice, in practice, is dictated by the authorities. Rarely a beneficiary opts for a particular type of asset on his own,[7] and remain contended with whatever is given to him. Moreover, it is not even possible for the programme implementers to prepare economically viable schemes for each and every beneficiary because of paucity of time, constraints of resources, both man power as well as financial.[8] Thus, in judging the effectiveness of IRDP assistance, in addition to the criterion of 'crossing the poverty line' one has to take into account the pre-assistance income of the beneficiary and the quantum of assistance or the value of the asset provided.

One of the studies[9] not only advocates for the consideration of the quantum of assistance for judging the effectiveness of IRDP assistance, but asserts that higher doses of investments should be given to the poorer families. Its line of thinking is based on the following analysis.

If Yb be the income of any given family before assistance, (3,500—Yb) is the distance the family has to cover to cross the poverty line.

Let I_i be the investment made for the family and K_i be the capital-output ratio (COR) of the scheme which has been offered to (or chosen by) the family.

Then I_i/K_i is the additional income generated by investment.[10]

If $I_i>(3{,}500-Yb)$, then the investment has succeeded in pushing the family above the poverty line.

In other words, $I_i/K_i/(3{,}500-Yb)>1$ or $I_i/K_i.1/(3{,}500-Yb)>1$ for the family to cross the poverty line.

This means that atleast one of the following three conditions has to be fulfilled if the family were to cross the poverty line :

(1) higher investment (I_i),

(2) low capital-output ratio (K_i), and

(3) family income being very near the poverty line, that is, smaller (3500—Yb).

Since according to the IRDP guidelines, those families whose (3,500—Yb) is the highest have to be chosen for assistance, chances of these families crossing the poverty line would depend on higher values of I_i and/or lower values of K_i. It is, however, not possible to influence K_i to a significant extent in the short run. The only variable well within the control of planners is I_i. Thus, it is only by fairly high investments that we can hope to push relatively poor families above the poverty line.

It may also be argued the other way, that higher investments to the lower income categories may be detrimental to the generation of additional income because high-investment assets are normally more difficult to maintain. The 'backwash' effects of such investments are likely to be greater than the 'spread' effects, since most of the investments are initially absorbed in maintaining a certain level of infrastructural sustenance.[11] Such investments require greater care and attention and the diffusion effects of such investments have to be closely monitored. In the absence of adequate followup, these investments rarely produce the desired results.[12]

Apart from the fact that crossing the poverty line criterion for judging the effectiveness of IRDP assistance is debatable, the very basis of the concept of poverty line can be put to question.[13] However, there has to be a line drawn out between those who are poor and those who are not on the basis of a standardised norm, universally acceptable, and the planners have had to adhere to certain norms, which they have done while defining the poverty line. To a beneficiary, however, poverty line, or a concept of the sort, is a misnomer. His perception of success remains within the confines of his 'self' and 'family'. If by virtue of an incremental income from IRDP assistance, he is able to increase his frequency of meals in a day or to improve relatively the quality of food, he will consider himself better off. Or if he is able to replace an old thatch on the roof of his house, or to afford to buy a slate for his child, he will again be said to have improved his economic condition by his fellow counterpart. In other words, each beneficiary family may have its own perception of poverty line, depending upon the intensity of its own destitution. This may have very little to do with an official poverty line however sophisticated its measurements are and however important it may be for the policy makers and programme planners. In view of this reasoning, it will be useful to see the income generation effects of the IRD programme, before going into the broader objective of IRDP of crossing the poverty line.

Income Generation from IRDP

The distribution of annual net income from assets is presented in table 6.1. The table shows that the percentage share of sample beneficiaries in whose case the asset did not generate any income was as high as 22 at the national level, which indicates that nearly one-fourth of the IRDP assets have not generated any income at all. This is a situation which calls for a serious rethinking on the part of the implementers of the IRD programme. This percentage varied across the states, varying from as high as 57 per cent in Manipur to nil in Sikkim and Tripura. Other states where this percentage was quite high were Nagaland (55 per cent), Haryana (49 per cent), Meghalaya (47 per cent) and Rajasthan (46 per cent). The fact that almost half of the IRDP assets were not generating any income in these states shows that there is something seriously wrong with the implementation of IRDP. It would be interesting to see the type of relationship these non-income generating states have with 'not-intact' asset cases (refer table 5.8) of the previous chapter). There appeared to be a close positive relationship between the two. In Manipur where 57 per cent of assets did not generate any income, the percentage of not-intact assets was as high as 67. In Nagaland where 55 per cent of assets did not generate any income, the percentage of not-intact assets was 30. Similar was the case with Haryana. Meghalaya and Rajasthan where the percentages were 55, 67 and 53 respectively. There were 4 states with less than 10 per cent cases of zero income assets. They were Gujarat (5 per cent), West Bengal (3 per cent), and Sikkim and Tripura (nil each). The corresponding 'asset not-intact' cases in these states were Gujarat (13 per cent), West Bengal (3 per cent), and Sikkim and Tripura (nil each).

The table also shows that 78 per cent of the beneficiaries at the national level owned assets which generated income between Re. 1 and Rs. 2,000 or above, out of which 10 per

Table 6.1

Income from Asset

(in Rupees)

State	0	1-500	501-1,000	1,001-2,000	>2000	Total
1	2	3	4	5	6	7
Andhra Pradesh	13	4	11	22	50	100
Assam	37	15	15	10	23	100
Bihar	17	13	35	24	11	100
Gujarat	5	6	28	44	17	100
Haryana	49	2	18	16	15	100
Himachal Pradesh	25	8	9	18	30	100
Jammu and Kashmir	15	1	9	27	47	100
Karnataka	17	24	22	22	15	100
Kerala	15	25	29	24	7	100
Madhya Pradesh	21	7	13	26	33	100
Maharashtra	16	12	18	20	34	100
Manipur	57	21	11	7	4	100

Meghalaya	47	15	16	8	14	100
Nagaland	55	6	10	10	9	100
Orissa	28	10	11	17	34	100
Punjab	22	0	6	30	42	100
Rajasthan	46	14	13	17	10	100
Sikkim	0	0	15	80	5	100
Tamil Nadu	32	6	14	23	25	100
Tripura	0	0	3	6	85	100
Uttar Pradesh	13	4	18	40	25	100
West Bengal	3	6	9	18	64	100
Union Territories	22	5	14	29	30	100
National average	22	10	17	24	27	100

Table 6.2

Percentage Increase in Family Income

State	*0*	*1-25*	*26-50*	*51-100*	*100*	*Total*
1	*2*	*3*	*4*	*5*	*6*	*7*
Andhra Pradesh	9	21	20	35	15	100
Assam	17	30	28	17	8	100
Bihar	18	23	31	18	10	100
Gujarat	2	14	39	43	2	100
Haryana	92	5	2	0	1	100
Himachal Pradesh	6	4	7	18	65	100
Jammu and Kashmir	23	10	9	26	32	100
Karnataka	42	16	10	15	17	100
Kerala	22	19	25	17	17	100
Madhya Pradesh	5	23	33	30	9	100
Maharashtra	10	19	18	33	20	100
Manipur	5	18	22	48	7	100

Meghalaya	38	22	8	15	17	100
Nagaland	15	40	20	5	20	100
Orissa	5	18	30	26	21	100
Punjab	8	9	23	35	15	100
Rajasthan	15	16	20	29	20	100
Sikkim	9	20	5	51	15	100
Tamil Nadu	16	20	20	28	12	100
Tripura	2	12	28	49	9	100
Uttar Pradesh	37	23	16	14	10	100
West Bengal	20	28	27	20	5	100
Union Territories	18	30	16	28	8	100
National average	20	23	23	23	14	100

cent were from the income bracket Re. 1-500, 17 per cent from the income bracket Rs. 501-1,000, 24 per cent from the income bracket Rs. 1,001-2,000 and 27 per cent with income above Rs. 2,000. In this context, it may be recalled that the Sixth Plan outlay of Rs. 4,500 crore to assist 15 million beneficiaries (that is, at the average rate of Rs. 3,000 per beneficiary) on the assumption of an incremental capital-output ratio (ICOR) of 1.5 implied that on the average, the income increment per family will be Rs. 2,000. The evaluation studies conducted during the Sixth Plan had revealed that an ICOR of 1.5 is too optimistic even for the IRD programme,[14] and that in reality it was close to 3. As a consequence, the ICOR assumed for the Seventh Plan is 2.7. In the light of these facts, the finding that half of the beneficiaries (51 per cent to be exact) had an income of more than Rs. 1,000 from the assets is indeed commendable, and that too after reckoning the fact that in 28 per cent cases the assets were not intact. The picture showed a lot of variation across the states so far as income from the IRDP is concerned. The highest percentage of cases with income upto Rs. 500 was in Kerals (25 per cent) and the lowest was in Punjab, Sikkim and Tripura (nil in all the three states). Whereas in Punjab, 22 per cent of the assets generated no income, in Sikkim and Tripura all incomes generated were above Rs. 500. In the Rs. 501-1,000 income generation category, there were 35 per cent assets in Bihar, on the one hand, to 6 per cent in Punjab on the other. It will be interesting to see the states where there are highest and lowest number of assets in the income category of Rs. 1,001-2,000 and in the income category of more than Rs. 2,000. Whereas in the former, the state with the highest percentage of beneficiaries was Sikkim (80 per cent) and the lowest was Manipur and Tripura (7 per cent each), in the latter category (that is, above Rs. 2,000), there were 85 per cent beneficiaries in Tripura to a low of 4 per cent in Manipur. If we combine the two categories and see the performance of the states where the assets generated an income of more than Rs. 1,000, we find that the best performance was from Tripura (92 per cent), Sikkim (85 per cent) and West Bengal (82 per cent). The states with an income generation of more than Rs. 1,000 in more than 50 per cent cases were Andhra Pradesh, Gujarat, Jammu and Kashmir, Madhya Pradesh, Maharashtra, Orissa, Punjab, Sikkim, Uttar Pradesh, West Bengal and the Union Territories. These states can be said to have performed well in terms of income generation from IRDP assistance. However, whether such an income generation would be sustained over a period of time, is a thing to be watched.[15]

An increase in income from IRDP assistance would not necessarily mean an increase in the total family income of the beneficiary. While the former may be a source of immediate relief to the beneficiary, it is the latter which counts for his ultimate welfare. An IRDP asset might have changed the status of a beneficiary from a wage-earner to a self-employed without substantially changing the family income. It may be a highly successful case of IRDP assistance in terms of the absolute income generated by the asset, but may not necessarily improve the net disposable income of the family. A more sensitive measure of improvement in the levels of living may be the percentage increase in the family income preferably ofter correcting for price changes. Besides IRDP assistance, there could be other factors also which might have affected the incomes of the families. In fact, for a more scientific analysis, one should have observed the differences in income during the same period of a 'control group' of families which were identical to the assisted sample beneficiaries, except for the IRDP assistance.[16] However, the changes in incomes of the assisted families, by and large, can be attributed to IRDP assistance.[17]

The percentage increase in family income is given in table 6.2. The table shows that at the national level there was no increase in family income after IRDP assistance in 20 per cent cases. There could be several reasons for this. If the beneficiary did not get the asset at all or if the asset was totally defective or if it got destroyed for lack of adequate care or for any other reason, no income would be generated. The process of acquiring the IRDP asset might have involved other costs that had to be incurred by the beneficiary, or the opportunity cost of IRDP might be reduced income from other sources, say wage labour. Under such conditions, if the IRDP asset does not generate any income the family income might even decline.[18] Percentage of cases with no increase in family income varied across the states. No increase in family income was reported from 92 per cent beneficiaries in Haryana, which goes to show that IRDP assistance in this state has been absolutely of no avail. The percentage of such cases was also high in Karnataka (42 per cent), Meghalaya (38 per cent) and Uttar Pradesh (37 per cent). The state governments should look into the reasons for such high percentage of cases of households where the family income did not increase or who became even worse off after the IRDP assistance. Out of the remaining 80 per cent beneficiaries who experienced an increase in family income during the post-assistance period, 20 per cent had an increase of upto 25 per cent of the pre-assistance income, 23 per cent had an increase between 26 and 50 per cent, another 23 per cent had an increase between 51 and 100 per cent and the remaining 14 per cent of the beneficiaries experienced more than 100 per cent increase in the family income from IRDP assistance. Doubling of the family income as a result of IRDP assistance, irrespective of the pre-assistance income level might have had a profound impact on the overall well-being of the family. Even an increase of more than 50 per cent in the family income over the pre-assistance income within a short period can be deemed to be of great significance from the viewpoint of the family's welfare. From the table it can be seen that 37 per cent of the beneficiaries at the national level experienced more than 50 per cent increase in the family income, irrespective of the value of assets given to them, which can be considered to be a significant gain. Thus, the IRDP assistance can be said to have been fruitful and the IRD programme successful among these families. The percentage of such families within the states was 50 in Andhra Pradesh, 83 in Himachal Pradesh, 58 in Jammu and Kashmir, 53 in Maharashtra, 55 in Manipur, 50 in Punjab, 66 in Sikkim and 58 in Tripura.

Crossing the Poverty Line

The income accruing from the IRDP asset measures the direct income generation impact of the beneficiary and is relevant for working out the productivity of the asset and estimating the incremental capital-output ratios (ICORs). The increment in the family income from all sources (including the asset) as a proportion of the pre-assistance income measures the total welfare effect of the programme on the beneficiary family. It is the net increment in family income in relation to the pre-assistance level of income which is of relevance. However, the criterion of crossing the poverty line should not be totally ignored in judging the effectiveness of IRDP assistance, if it goes hand in hand with the other criteria.[20] Another criticism of crossing the poverty line criterion is that throughout the Sixth Plan, it ignored the price changes or the inflation factor, which should have been incorporated in the poverty line. As a result, even when the data for this survey was collected, the poverty line remained at Rs. 3,500 for the purpose of IRDP assistance, when the actual poverty line had become Rs. 6,400.[21]

The percentage of eligible beneficiaries who have crossed the poverty line of Rs. 3,500 and Rs. 6,400 are presented in table 6.3. About 48 per cent beneficiaries crossed the poverty line of Rs. 3,500 at the national level. Across the states, the percentage varied from nil in Sikkim and 2 in Haryana, to 100 in Tripura, 88 in Gujarat, 85 in Punjab and 72 in Manipur. With reference to the revised poverty line of Rs. 6,400, the percentage of beneficiaries crossing the poverty line came down drastically. At the national level, 5 per cent of the beneficiaries crossed the new poverty line. The statewise figures varied from nil each in Tripura and the Union Territories to 26 in Himachal Pradesh and 18 in Jammu and Kashmir.

The factors that determine the proportion of beneficiaries who cross the poverty line are: (1) pre-assistance level of income of the beneficiary, (2) quantum of assistance, and (3) the actual incremental capital-output ratios (ICORs). It was not possible to calculate the ICOR for individual schemes. Similarly, the quantum of assistance received by individual

Table 6.3

Percentage of Persons with Initial Income less than Rs. 3,500 crossing the Poverty Line

State	*Poverty Line Rs. 3,500*	*Poverty Line Rs. 6,400*
Andhra Pradesh	68	5
Assam	63	2
Bihar	32	2
Gujarat	81	2
Haryana	2	1
Himachal Pradesh	70	26
Jammu and Kashmir	58	18
Karnataka	23	4
Kerala	40	3
Madhya Pradesh	45	3
Maharashtra	53	5
Manipur	72	3
Meghalaya	23	5
Nagaland	50	7
Orissa	43	5
Punjab	95	12
Rajasthan	45	5
Sikkim	0	10
Tamil Nadu	44	1
Tripura	100	0
Uttar Pradesh	45	5
West Bengal	56	7
Union Territories	57	0
National average	48	5

beneficiaries has not been tabulated at the all India level in the main findings of the concurrent evaluation. The only variable that can be examined with respect to crossing the poverty line is the pre-assistance income of the beneficiary, which has been presented in table 5.1 of the previous chapter. A comparison of this table with table 6.3 will enable us to establish a link between the level of pre-assistance income and crossing the poverty line. For our purpose, only those beneficiaries, whose pre-assistance incomes are upto Rs. 3,500 are relevant. Since these beneficiaries are classified into two groups, viz., those with income upto Rs. 2,266 and those with income between Rs. 2,266 and Rs. 3,500, the relative shares in the groups can be compared with the percentages crossing the poverty line, as given in table 6.3. By and large, it can be seen that a higher percentage of beneficiaries crossed the poverty line from those states where the shares of eligible beneficiaries from the income group Rs. 2,266 to 3,500 were higher. Thus, for example, in Andhra Pradesh, Assam, Gujarat, Jammu and Kashmir, Punjab and several others, the percentage of beneficiaries who crossed the poverty line of Rs. 3,500 was higher, since in these states the percentage of eligible beneficiaries from the income group Rs. 2,266 to Rs. 3,500 was much higher than from the income group Re. 1-2,265. Similarly, in Sikkim and Meghalaya the percentage of beneficiaries crossing the poverty line of Rs. 3,500 was lower since the percentage of eligible beneficiaries from the income group Rs. 2,266 to Rs. 3,500 in these states was lower than from the income group Re. 1-2,265. This data justifiably supports the view that it is easier for a beneficiary on the brink of poverty line to cross the poverty barrier than for a beneficiary far away from it, although his performance from the IRDP might have been better than the performance of the former. It also corroborates the view expressed by a few researchers that it is not only 'crossing the poverty line' criterion which determines the success/failure of IRDP assistance, and that the IRD programme has no relevance for beneficiaries who have not been able to cross the poverty line. This indeed should be an important consideration for IRDP planning.

Notes and References

1. Subbarao has vehemently criticised the criterion of poverty line income to evaluate the performance of IRDP. According to him, crossing the poverty line depends on a number of factors which should be taken care of while evaluating the performance of IRDP. Kurien also is of the view that crossing the poverty line should not be the sole criterion for evaluating the performance of IRDP.
2. Even Rath has treated the IRDP assistance to beneficiaries who could not cross the poverty line as a sheer wastage. Although Kurien is of the view that the performance of IRDP should not be evaluated solely on crossing the poverty line criterion, he justifies the stand of the evaluators in taking this single criterion on the ground that this has been the criterion adopted by the planners during the Sixth Plan and that the evaluators were strictly following the stated criterion.
3. It is, however, wrong to assume that the ICOR of an asset belonging to a destitute will be the same as that of the ICOR of the same asset belonging to a poor.
4. Such a category has a weaker backward as well as forward linkage, in comparison to their relatively 'better off' counterparts. We are discussing here in the context of a beneficiary who is being viewed within the boundaries of the poverty line income, and even 'better off' are those who are below the poverty line.
5. Small farmers too can benefit from the IRDP schemes if they have an annual income below the poverty line income.
6. Assets with larger outlays like pumpsets or tubewells have greater cost-efficiency, and hence a greater ICOR.
7. Beneficiary's own choice in the selection of asset can be mostly exercised in land-based activities or in tertiary sector activities.
8. The ideal situation would have been the one where an economically viable scheme was prepared for individual beneficiary, based on the 'need-based strategy' and depending upon his socio-economic condition as well as the infrastructural facilities available with him. This would definitely involve greater cost, more time and of course, some degree of motivation to the implementers of IRDP.
9. Report of the Institute of Financial Management and Research: "An economic assessment of poverty eradication and rural unemployment alleviation programmes and their prospects", p. 49. Also see the IRDP evaluation report prepared by Programme

Evaluation Organisation, Planning Commission, Govt. of India, p. 133.

10. Since $K_i = I_i/y$ and $I_i = K_iY$, therefore $I_i/K_i = Y$.

11. Mohsin, Nadeem, "IRDP: some policy considerations," Southern Economist, Vol. 27, No. 5, July 1, 1988.

12. Mohsin, Nadeem, "IRDP: need for followup," abstract published in the Indian Journal of Agricultural Economics, Conference No., Part II, Oct.-Dec. 1986. Also see Mohsin, Nadeem, "Integrated rural development and poverty alleviatien," in Sharma and Gupta edited, Bihar: Stagnation Or Growth, Spectrum Publishing House, New Delhi, 1987.

13. The calorie requirement which constitutes the basis of the official poverty line has been a matter of controversy for the last two decades. Those who believe that 'man lives not by bread alone' want the poverty line to be stretched further to include other private consumption as well as public services like health, sanitation, education and other public utilities. This, however, involves an element of subjectivity and value judgement on the part of the beneficiary, which is difficult to quantify.

14. This refers to the IFMR, NABARD and PEO studies. The data for the three studies suggest that the capital-output ratio of 1.5, estimated by the Planning Commission is expected to hold good only in regions where sustained amount of investment in infrastructure was already incurred. The assumed ratio of 1.5 is clearly not realistic for the backward regions.

15. Income generation from IRDP assistance depends on a number of factors. It is not necessary that an asset performing well at one point of time may perform equally well at a different point of time.

16. Kurien, N.J., "IRDP: how relevant is it"?, Economic and Political Weekly, Dec. 26, 1987.

17. According to Kurien, apart from a few exceptions, in most cases, major changes in the economic status of the assisted families have been only due to the IRDP assistance. It is found that the benefits of even the other anti-poverty programmes like NREP and RLEGP go sparingly to IRDP beneficiaries. The empirical findings suggest that the various anti-poverty programmes are of a complementary nature rather than the same group of poor families getting benefits on a supplementary basis.

18. The IRDP asset might even lead to a decline in family income if the beneficiary has given up wage labour and incurred certain costs in procuring the asset.

19. In working out the net increment in family income in relation to the pre-assistance level of income, the income from the IRDP asset is deducted after netting the loan repayments.
20. The other criteria referred to are the ones discussed here, that is, the income generation from the IRDP asset criterion and the total increase in family income (from all sources) criterion.
21. According to the guidelines issued on IRDP, only those whose incomes were below Rs. 3,500 were eligible for assistance under the IRD programme.

7

Towards a Direct Attack on Poverty

Ever since the conception of IRDP, there has been a debate whether India's immediate need has been a short-term goal of poverty alleviation or a long-term objective of transforming the structure of rural society. The critics of the anti-poverty programmes consider it to be mere palliatives, devoid of providing a solution to the problem of the rural poor.[1] On the other hand, there are others who feel that it is only through the programmes of poverty alleviation that one can find a solution to the problems of the poor. The truth lies probably within the two extremes. Poverty alleviation programmes should be geared by intent to the improvement of the social and economic structure.[2] Devoid of such linkage they tend to become relief programmes which, though vital for the survival of the poor, may be inadequate for the purpose of rural development with a broader perspective.

Programmes which are effective in enabling an individual or a family to cross the poverty line, without a change in awareness or ability, are not necessarily the ones which are suitable, and even necessary, for changing the community structure in the desired direction. A programme of road construction, for example, can contribute to poverty alleviation but not to awareness building. It is in fact very difficult to construct and implement a programme which could lead to the enhancement of the ability and the creation of awareness of the rural poor. Such a programme, as has been the experience, is very difficult to implement. The change agent does not have the expertise or the experience to operate such programmes; they also attract opposition from vested interests and are therefore less successful. In fact, they often fail by the simple poverty alleviation criterion, although they might have been even marginally successful otherwise. A programme of rural development should, thus, be viewed from the objective of a direct attack on poverty. This attack has to be two-pronged: one which brings the poor above the poverty line in the short run and the other which brings about an overall transformation in the structure of the rural society.

The basic flaw in the IRD programme is in the selection of the beneficiary. Although the beneficiaries are to be selected in the gram sabha meeting, such a procedure is not always followed, leading to several cases of wrong identification. This is probably because of the excessive workload assigned to the programme, a target of 600 beneficiaries per block per year. The selection process should start with the consent of the poor.[3] Of course, this selection has to be rational, bearing in mind the objectives of the IRDP assistance. The selection committee should comprise of the BDO, the village mukhiya, the VLW and three persons from the village. The committee should be given sufficient time to select the beneficiaries.[4] The five man committee appointed for selection should be extremely strict, vigilant and objective.[5]

The choice of the scheme should, in practice, vest with the beneficiary, since it is he who will be using the asset for his family's welfare. In cases, where a beneficiary fails to exercise his choice,[6] he should be ably assisted by the VLW, the village mukhiya and the BDO, who should choose the asset for the beneficiary, taking into account the beneficiary's economic status, his aptitude and the infrastructural facilities at his disposal.

The identification of the poor as well as the choice of schemes are two critical components of the IRD programme.

Whereas wrong identification defeats the very purpose of IRDP, the wrong choice of schemes often results in the beneficiary's decision to dispose off the asset or in the actual loss of the asset. These cases have been often reported, as discussed in the earlier chapter. In order to make a proper selection of the poor as well as to select the asset of his choice, the implementers will have to have enough time at their disposal to avoid mistakes owing to paucity of time.

It is noticed that a lot of bungling takes place in the purchase of assets. One suggestion has been that the beneficiaries should be given cash in place of the actual asset, to avoid misappropriation of funds at different levels. Neither of the two, that is, cash given directly or asset purchased through a purchase committee, appears feasible in the present state of affairs. In fact, the latter, in all probability, would make things turn from bad to worse.[7] If the former procedure is undertaken with certain modifications, that is, the purchase committee is reconstituted, bunglings, to a large extent, can be avoided. Enough time should be given to the beneficiary to purchase the asset of his choice, and the liberty should be given to the beneficiary to make the purchase committee as democratic as possible. A purchase committee comprisiag of the block and bank official, could, if necessary, be extended to accommodate two or three other members of the beneficiary's choice. These members could be from the beneficiary's village or from other villages, but they should have the goodwill of the beneficiary. This procedure of purchasing the asset could mitigate the bunglings to a large extent.

The training and after care support input is also lacking to a great extent in the IRD programme. After care support should be provided to the beneficiaries by an IRDP extension specialist. This specialist should be based at the block level and should be closely in touch with the beneficiaries, in collaboration with the VLWs. The specialist should have undergone a rigorous training before being appointed at the respective blocks. He should also be expected to act as a liaison between the block and the beneficiary, delivering all pertinent information to the beneficiary. So far as the question of training is concerned, it is easy to suggest that the beneficiaries require adequate training in handling the asset. However, what should be the modus operandi of such a training is an issue, mostly ignored We are today constrained by our understanding of training needs at the grassroots level. Of late, there has been a spurt of training activity in the government, but obvious class and service considerations have only given preferential priority to officials well above the local level. In fact, the present thrust in training is marked by an unabashed concern for the career graph of officials far removed from the local level.[8] The training of IRDP beneficiaries is thus very much in the background. As it is, we have very little experience and even knowledge to design a training programme for the grassroots level. We do not know the technology of training as part of an instructional strategy, to meet even the perceived training needs. Do we rely on formal training or explore the alternatives of informal training? This is a question we should pose to ourselves. The task is stupendous but nevertheless within our reach. We need alert and perceptive trainers to formulate the alternative initiatives. We need training as an integral part of the IRDP strategy, to promote better utilisation of assets. The training aspect of the IRDP has thus to be considered in a wider perspective. While stressing on handling of assets, the scope and coverage of training has to be substantially enlarged. At the grassroots level, the local functionaries as well need to be trained. In fact, it could be a shared approach to learn and unlearn, to find out not only how a field-level programme can be performed better, but also why it is not being implemented. This approach may not only help in creating appropriate rapport between the local functionaries and the beneficiaries, but may also help the beneficiaries to help themselves through a better understanding of the programme implementation. It should be mentioned here that Vikas Patrika[9] should be distributed to each and every IRDP beneficiary to enable him understand better the different components of IRDP, especially the training aspect of the programme.

The absence of both vertical as well as horizontal linkages is another crucial area which needs a close examination. A very serious lacuna in the IRD programme is the missing link, both backwards and forwards, within a scheme. This link is so obviously absent that it has become one of the greatest bottlenecks for an IRDP beneficiary. In fact, the procurement of inputs at the right time and in adequate quality for an asset to produce the desired results has never been geared to the advantage of a beneficiary. Similar is the link of the product (from the IRDP asset) with the market. Two implications are clearly visible due to the absence of the backward and forward linkage. One, high production cost incurred on the asset, and two, unattractive price for the product.[10] The problem of uneasy access to inputs to the destitute and very very poor families is indeed old. It does not involve any controversy either. If a programme like the IRDP is to work under a system of uneasy access to inputs, it will be very difficult for such a programme to survive. Similarly, if the market system is beyond the control of a seller, he can at best look forward to a price which buyers are willing to pay and which would definitely be much lower than what he would expect. So far as the question of access to inputs is concerned, each and every beneficiary should be guaranteed access to all inputs required for generating income from the asset. Each and every IRDP scheme should have a well planned out input network which should be looked after by the local level functionaries. To take an example, suppose the scheme is that of providing a milch animal to a beneficiary; there would be several beneficiaries from among the villages in a block with a similar scheme. The most important inputs required for a milch animal would be a veterinary centre, providing free health services (for ascertaining quality product and in adequate quantity) and a feeding centre, providing adequate and quality feed. If these two centres are made available in a block,[11] they would cater to the needs of all the beneficiaries having milch animal as an asset.[12] Unless access to inputs is thought of in these terms for every individual scheme, backward linkages in IRDP cannot be guaranteed. Coming to the forward linkages, these too have to be planned out for every individual scheme. To continue with the example of a milch animal, the milk that is extracted from the cow needs to be transported immediately to the nearest collection centre. This centre should be located at a point where each and every beneficiary is able to reach within the shortest possible time. The centre should, in turn, carry milk to the respective markets. It should also issue cards to each beneficiary having a milch animal. The card should keep record of the quantity of milk collected from every beneficiary each day. The price of procuring this milk from the beneficiaries should be fixed by the respective state governments on behalf of the centre. This price should be only marginally lower than the price charged at the milk booths in cities where such centres are carrying the milk. The marginal difference in price should compensate for the costs on transportation plus the cost incurred on management at the two levels. The earnings of the beneficiary each day should be entered in the card. The beneficiary should sign his card each day that he deposits milk and verify if the entry in terms of quantity of milk deposited and the amount earned by him has been properly recorded. There should be a tendency on the part of the officials at the centre not to pay to the beneficiary his entire earnings of the day. In fact, he should be asked to save compulsorily unless his earnings have been low. The entire strategy planned out for a beneficiary with a milch animal can be planned out for other schemes as well.[13] It will be a task requiring adequate time and effort.

The horizontal integration in IRDP has been a subject of lot of criticism and debate. The controversy arises on the issue of wage-employment as well as self-employment. Rath argues that integration between wage-employment and self-employment is not necessary, for wage-employment alone can be the mainstay of the IRD programme.[14] According to Hirway, on the contrary, self-employment is the major form of employment in rural India.[15] However, there has to be an integration between the two, that is, self-employment programme (IRDP) should be linked with wage-employment programmes (NREP, RLEGP, etc.). For example, construction of roads, an NREP work, should go hand in hand with IRDP, and employment under NREP should be given to a member of the family belonging to the IRDP beneficiary, so that while the IRDP schemes are being launched, necessary linkages for these schemes are also being provided for.

The absence of vertical as well as horizontal integration has largely been a result of administrative lapses, implementers' apathy and lack of overall coordination. Programme identification, project formulation, resource allocation, implementation procedures, etc., figure prominently in the overall operational methodology designed to achieve integration.[16] The identification of the appropriate administrative machinery, its acceptance by concerned agencies and operationalisation become crucial elements of the whole policy package. The requirement of vertical and horizontal integration to be fulfilled simultaneously presupposes a high degree of administrative sophistication which, if not present, may complicate the implementation of the IRD programme. If the different forums devised for coordination become the focul points for genuine collaboration over a period of time, the prevailing administrative shortcoming should be overcome. The integration of IRDP as a method finds favour with some experts who consider it more as a method of action than a subject by itself requiring action.[17]

It is true that IRDP has not been able to give satisfactory results, largely owing to the lack of integration within the different components of the programme and also with other programmes which, in itself, has been on account of administrative failures. The basic mistake has probably been the hurried expansion of the programme to cover the entire rural areas at the beginning of the Sixth Plan. It was a bit too much to expect of a programme as complicated as IRDP to be expanded to such an extent within such a short time.[18] Considering the mammoth dimensions of IRDP, in terms of the number of beneficiaries convered and the various stages of planning and implementation according to the guidelines, no doubt, the bureaucratic limits have been reached during the

Sixth Plan in a literal sense and perhaps more so in a logical sense.[19] This could be an important reason why the Seventh Plan has given emphasis on people's involvement in planning, implementation and monitoring of IRDP. Another reason why the involvement of bureaucracy in IRDP is not to the extent desired is the system of regular transfers and postings. By the time a deputy development commissioner (DDC), for example, examines the past loopholes in the implementation of the programme and tries to launch it after proper rectification, he is transferred. IRDP is a programme which requires vigil at the district level, because it is from here that decentralisation in the programme implementation actually begins.[20] The bureaucratic machinery, as a result, neither has the will nor the inclination to take interest in the long-term impact of the programme. Its only concern centres around target fulfilment, since the results of IRDP are assessed in quantitative terms.[21]

The greatest achievement of IRDP has been its contribution to awareness building in whatever little measure it has been able to. Perhaps, rural poor, who are still unaware of the fact that there is a programme to alleviate poverty can now be singled out from almost every Indian village. If this programme is properly integrated with other poverty alleviation programmes and minimum needs programme like primary education, health, nutrition, water supply and sanitation, etc., the long-term effects of IRDP would be far greater. The question of poverty cannot be tackled only by providing to cow here and a buffalow there. It has to be examined in a much broader perspective.

The foremost reason for this unfortunate state of affairs is that the people themselves have no place in rural development; every available inch is occupied by the bureaucracy.[22] The community which was once central to the rural development strategy, is now peripheral to it. A vast development bureaucracy has replaced elected Panchayats.[23] It may be recalled that Panchayats were brought in due to the failure of the Community Development Programme in the fifties.

Panchayati Raj was then fashioned to provide an institutional base for the people's active involvement in the development effort in their respective villages, blocks and districts. The Panchayati Raj system, hailed as pivotal both to development and democratic policy, was inaugurated by Nehru twenty-five years ago. However, it had an end before it could actually begin. This is evident from the fact that no elections have been held to village Panchayats in most states in the last fifteen years or so. Even where elections have been held, like in Rajasthan, the Panchayats have not been endowed with any worthwhile development functions and resources. Unless the powers of the Panchayats are restored, we cannot expect anything in terms of people's involvement and participation.[24]

If the goal of a direct attack on mass poverty is to be attained seriously, it would require tough decisions. To begin with, it would require entirely new alliances to implement the new policies.[25] The fact is that development administration is more solidly allied with the rural rich than with the poor.[26] At the political level, an alliance has to be made between those interest groups which stand for redistribution of income and for reaching the poorer sections of the society.[27] Such an alliance, in the ultimate analysis, must embrace the willing and enthusiastic participation of the poor. The popular story about the IRDP, as mentioned earlier, is that the same buffalo goes again and again to a number of recipients yielding more subsidies than milk.[28] The MLAs and MPs, who once were obliged to lend support to Panchayats in their own electoral interest, are also, by and large, backing up the alliance of the administration with the rural rich. An alternate alliance between the poor and the administration is difficult to form. It often requires a broad-based mass movement to mobilise the energies of the people, which has not been possible to this day in India.

The essence of the new development strategies towards a direct attack on mass poverty are, in fact, fundamental institutional reforms. At the heart of these reforms is a change in the existing control over the means of production and access to key services. Normally, the rich exercise enormous economic power within these systems, because they control most of the means of production in the society, such as land and capital. That is why land reforms has become the key element in any institutional reforms. Unfortunately, land reforms has yet to be implemented effectively in most of the states of the country. Alongwith institutional reforms in the control over the means of production, there must also be a change in the distribution of public services to the poorest sections of the society. In the last analysis, it is the equality of opportunity, not the equality of income, which is decisive for future growth in the backward rural areas. The poor are denied this equality of opportunity, not only because of the prevailing income distribution, but principally because they have an unequal access to education, credit system, public utilities and other services. Their initial poverty, therefore, becomes a formidable handicap in improving their future conditions.

One of the themes in the new development strategies, which has probably gained the most favour with development planners and policy makers, is the concept of basic human needs. It is generally accepted by now that in poor societies production planning should initially be geared to the satisfaction of basic needs. There are atleast three steps that are essential for formulating a need-oriented development strategy. First, the target groups must be defined with a good deal of precision (after collecting the necessary data on the profile of poverty) and identified accordingly. Second, quantitative studies must be undertaken to estimate the population which is below the minimum human needs, and an estimate made regarding the production and investment targets which should be set to meet these consumption targets over a defined period of time. Third, the necessary instruments of implementation should be defined to indicate how these consumption targets are to be realised in a market. There is no evidence at present that these steps are being seriously pursued in the context of a commitment to a direct attack on mass poverty. Under the present circumstance, therefore, the most concrete suggestion that can be made is to call a complete halt to the officially administered poverty alleviation and rural development programmes until we are ready to rely on the community and its elected bodies to shoulder the main burden of local government. Without this, development with a direct attack on mass poverty would be a far cry. This suggestion should be seriously considered before finalising the Eighth Plan.

Notes and References

1. Rao, V.M., "Impact of IRDP on village structure", Economic and Political Weekly, March 28, 1987.
2. Dantwala, M.L., "Discussion on 'IRDP and village structure'", Economic and Political Weekly, May 30, 1987, p. 858.
3. In such a situation, it would be likely that the entire village turns up for IRDP assistance claiming themselves to be the genuine poor.
4. Target consciousness in IRDP assistance leads to hasty decisions which result in wrong identification. Also hurried decisions give greater scope to the manipulators.
5. There could be a tendency on the part of the implementers to deliberately select beneficiaries who are above the poverty line, so that when it comes to the evaluation of IRDP performance, based as it is, on the poverty line criterion, the implementers can claim to have achieved a reasonable degree of success.
6. There will be very many cases where the beneficiary will not be able to exercise his choice owing to his illiteracy, unawareness and ignorance about the programme.
7. The beneficiary's perception of economic rationality is absolutely different from the implementer's perception. A beneficiary should be appreciated (with his limited knowledge and awareness) if he considers his son's marriage, for example, a subject of economic rationality. He is, as a matter of fact, governed by his immediate needs and does not want to involve himself in the intricacies of the concept of poverty line or incremental capital-output ratio, etc.
8. Saxena, A.P., "Concurrent evaluation of IRDP: selected aspects for administrative followup", Economic and Political Weekly, Sept. 26, 1987.

9. The Vikas Patrika, by and large, has an ornamental value. In Bihar, it has been lying in the almirahs of the block offices and in a very few cases have these booklets been distributed to the beneficiaries.
10. Due to lack of beneficiaries' control on prices, the beneficiaries have to make distress sales, which largely results from the exploitation they have to face in the market. The lack of control or market results in what can be termed as 'exploitative prices'.
11. One veterinary centre and one feeding centre in each block would take care of all the beneficiaries within a block. The centres would have to be well-equipped and manned by experts in their own fields. Loyalty towards duty would be a precondition for manning these centres.
12. Of course, it would be the duty of the local level functionaries to motivate the beneficiaries to utilise the services of these centres in order to make the best use of the IRDP assets.
13. One would have to consult specialists to plan out similar strategies for different schemes and if such strategies are formulated and implemented, IRDP schemes would certainly start showing improvements.
14. Rath, Nilkantha, "Garibi hatao: can IRDP do it", Economic and Political Weekly, Feb. 9, 1985, p. 238.
15. Refer to the discussion by Indira Hirway, Economic and Political Weekly, March 30, 1985, p. 561.
16. Hye, H.A., Integrated Approaches to Rural Development, Sterling Publishers, Privated Limited, New Delhi, 1986.
17. See Guy Hunter (ed.), Agricultural Development and the Rural Poor, Overseas Development Institute, London, 1978, p. 98.
18. Although, setting of targets always leads to better results, the time span of setting the target needs always to be considered in order to accommodate for the elimination of bottlenecks in the implementation procedure.
19. Kurien, N.J., "IRDP: how relevant is it ?", Economic and Political Weekly, Dec. 26, 1987, p. A-173.
20. Although in practice, such a decentralisation is not to be seen.
21. The results are assessed in terms of expenditure incurred and physical achievements in terms of numbers, irrespective of the physical quality of the achievements. The lesser the gap between target and achievement, the better is deemed to be the performance.
22. Jain, L.C. et. al., Grass Without Roots: Rural Development Through Government Auspices, Sage Publications, New Delhi, 1985, p. 197.

23. Panchayat refers to an assembly of the representatives of the local people.
24. Perhaps no exercise on rural development research is complete without prescribing for people's active participation and involvement, and as such they have become stereotypes.
25. Haq, Mahbub Ul, The Poverty Curtain: Choices for the Third World, Oxford University Press, New Delhi, 1976, p. 66.
26. According to Jain, the combination of the rural rich and the bureaucracy is formidable, fed as it is, on mounting corruption, claiming 50 to 80 per cent of the huge programme funds earmarked for the poor.
27. It must be realised that launching a direct attack on poverty is primarily a political and not a technocratic or a bureaucratic decision.
28. Op. cit. (22), p. 206.

Index

P

R

S

T

U

V

W